ECONOMIC GROWTH VERSUS THE ENVIRONMENT

Economic Growth versus the Environment

RICHARD LECOMBER

Lecturer in Economics, University of Bristol

A HALSTED PRESS BOOK

JOHN WILEY & SONS
New York

First published in the United Kingdom 1975 by
The Macmillan Press Ltd

Published in the U.S.A. by
Halsted Press, a Division of
John Wiley & Sons, Inc.
New York

Printed in Great Britain

Library of Congress Cataloging in Publication Data

Lecomber, J   R   C
    Economic growth versus the environment.

    "A Halsted Press book."
    Bibliography: p.
    1. Economic development—Social aspects.
2. Environmental policy. 3. Externalities (Economics) I. Title.
HD82. L329   1975   301.31   75–5605
    ISBN 0 470–52100–7

Contents

Acknowledgements

Warm thanks are due to David Pearce of the University of Leicester and Michael Common of the University of Southampton for valuable comments on an earlier draft, to Marjorie Lunt for struggling so patiently with my appalling handwriting, and to my wife for help, sympathy and encouragement throughout.

1 Introduction

The purpose of this book is to illumine a controversy – or rather that group of related controversies which have become entangled together under the general catch-phrase 'growth versus environment'.

'Growth' and 'environment' are very different sorts of concepts, in truth barely compatible. 'Growth' refers to the growth rate of some national accounting aggregate, usually the Gross National Product (G.N.P.). It is thus a precise concept, operationally defined and capable, in principle at least, of exact measurement. This is its strength – and also its weakness. Items which cannot satisfactorily be measured must of necessity be excluded, and thus it remains to be established whether a high G.N.P. is preferable to a low one.

By contrast, 'environment' and similar expressions are broad, vague, not reducible to single numbers and difficult to define with any precision. Unlike G.N.P., environmental quality is an essentially normative concept.

Another important difference, and a source of much confusion, is that whereas growth is a *dynamic* concept (a rate of change over time) environment is a *static* one. Or, as Heller [21] prefers to put it, growth is a means to an end (high output and hence high consumption), while environmental quality is an end in itself.

By growth we shall mean, in accordance with popular usage, the growth in G.N.P., measured over a few years, let us say a decade. Growth in this sense is unquestionably a central objective of policy in all countries. A very prominent economist (Harrod [99]) recently wrote 'Economic growth is the grand objective. It is the aim of economic policy as a whole.'

However, notwithstanding the exaggerated panegyrics on growth which flow so wantonly from the mouths of politicians and even some economists, it is not the only aim. Progressive

9

income tax, building regulations, the provision of geriatric care and of arts courses in universities, Factory Acts, Green Belt policies – to take a few examples at random – are, all of them, injurious to growth in G.N.P. These represent substantial concessions to preferences and values not adequately reflected in the growth statistic and a partial acceptance, at least, of the kinds of arguments advanced by the anti-growth school. Nevertheless, the quest for growth still exerts a powerful influence over socio-economic policy, which many consider excessive.

There is however one occasion when an increase in the growth rate is generally welcome – namely in a depression.[1] However its main virtue in such a context lies not so much in the additional output produced as in the alleviation of the social distress caused by unemployment. It may have costs too, in terms of inflation or balance-of-payments problems, but these are not the sort of costs with which we are concerned in this book. Such a means of achieving growth can, in any case, be only temporary: as soon as full employment is reached, growth can be raised only by sacrificing something else; even the dash to full employment may be achieved in many ways, with the accent on consumption or investment, on material goods or environmental improvement. These are the sorts of choices with which this book is concerned. The easiest way to focus attention on allocational choices is to assume full employment.

Growth may also be achieved by increases in population, e.g. through immigration. But since the increased output has to be shared between more people this is not necessarily advantageous. Since our concern is with economic rather than demographic growth, we shall assume the latter to be exogenously given.

The argument for growth is a straightforward one. G.N.P. is a measure of the achievement of the economic system in its (presumed) main aim, the production of goods and services. Growth is the means by which a higher output is achieved. 'Whatever a nation's goals – more help for the poor countries of the world, stronger defences, a larger public sector, a larger share of output for under-privileged persons at home – they can most easily be

[1] Likewise it is sometimes suggested that environmental policies (especially zero growth) may create unemployment. Reasons for rejecting this view are given in Chapter 6.

10

achieved by providing more resources through the growth of available output per head' [26].

Nevertheless, many environmentalists, regarding 'noise, smoke, pollution and the destruction of wild life and natural beauty, that follow in the wake of expanding industry and communication' consider 'that the continued pursuit of economic growth by western societies is more likely on balance to reduce rather than increase social welfare' [28].[1] 'Economic growth in terms of the gross national product is eroding the quality of life' [70].

Pro-growth writers, however, tend to deny the existence of a conflict. 'The mistake of the anti-growth men is to blame economic growth *per se* for the misdirection of economic growth' [30]. Indeed 'a rising G.N.P. will enable a nation more easily to bear the costs of eliminating pollution' [22].

A rather different argument is that medium-term growth is at the expense of the longer term. For a high level of output involves a rapid depletion of natural resources, a build-up of damaging wastes and a progressive interference with the eco-system. This puts at risk not only amenity but conventional economic output. 'If the present growth trends in world population, industrialisation, pollution, food production and resource depletion continue unchanged, the limits to growth on this planet will be reached sometime within the next hundred years. The most probable result will be a rather sudden and uncontrollable decline in both population and industrial capacity' [49].

Optimists have dismissed such prognostications with scorn as 'pseudo-science' [47], 'brazen impudent . . . nonsense . . . that nobody could possibly take seriously' [50]. 'In economic terms, the earth's resources seem to be becoming more plentiful' [47]. 'The nightmare of a day of reckoning when, for example, fossil

---

[1] In his wide-ranging critique, *The Costs of Economic Growth* [28], Mishan complains also of 'the obsolescence of skills, of knowledge and of culture', 'the tedium of repetitive work in modern industry', 'the unending scramble for material rewards and public recognition', 'the growing impatience and tenseness of people', 'the breakdown of communications between generations', 'the weakening of the moral props of an already disintegrating society', the increasing 'cynicism' and 'crime . . . in particular robbery with violence'.

fuels are forever gone seems to be based on failure to recognize the existing and future possibilities of substitute materials and processes' [30].

This controversy will be explored in Chapter 4.

In Chapter 5 we consider specific policies for protecting the environment. The growth-men admit that 'possible abuse of public natural resources is a . . . serious problem. [But] zero economic growth is a blunt instrument for cleaner air, prodigiously expensive and probably ineffectual' [30]. 'The way to control pollution is to control pollution not growth' [32]. 'The pollution problem is a simple matter of correcting a minor resource misallocation by means of pollution charges' [50].

But many environmentalists dispute the efficacy of conventional approaches. 'Pollution charges are not enough' [76]. 'Traditional cost-benefit calculus is not simply misleading but actually serves as an institutionalized cloak for large-scale spoliation' [72].

In Chapter 6 we examine the acrimonious disputes between growth-men and environmentalists over the distributional consequences of their proposals.

Growth-men claim that 'the richer and faster growing an economy is the more successful [it is] in promoting equality' [26] and suggest that 'most of the people who are currently anti-growth are motivated by middle-class value judgements' [15] and 'indifferent to the needs of ordinary people' [18].

Environmentalists disagree. 'Amenity-promoting legislation would tend to benefit the poor more than the rich . . . the rich can escape pollution, for the richer a man the wider is his choice of neighbourhood; [anyway] regressive effects . . . could . . . be corrected by taxes' [28]. 'The process of growth, as it is occurring today, is inexorably widening the absolute gap between the rich and the poor nations of the world' [49].

Many of the controversies in this book revolve around inadequacies in G.N.P. as an index of welfare. Accordingly in the Appendix we examine two attempts to construct a more satisfactory measure.

2 G.N.P. versus Environmental Services

Growth is desired not as an end in itself, but because it leads to a high level of output. Similarly pollution and the like are related less to growth itself as to the level of output that is thereby achieved.[1] Consequently it will greatly assist the clarity of the discussion if we begin by examining the static conflict between G.N.P. and associated environmental effects.

To focus on the essentials of this conflict, a number of simplifying assumptions will be made:

(i) The economy will be assumed to be in *static equilibrium*. Output equals consumption and there is no progressive environmental deterioration. This assumption will be relaxed in Chapter 3.

(ii) Since we are not concerned with international problems, we shall assume the economy *closed*. Hence G.N.P. equals G.D.P. (equals consumption) and output equals income. Certain international aspects of the growth–environment conflict will be considered briefly in Chapter 6.

(iii) Since we are not initially concerned with distributional issues, we shall assume the population to be endowed with *identical preferences, capacities and stocks of wealth*. This allows us to use community indifference curves unambiguously. This drastic assumption will be relaxed when consideration is given to the important issue of distribution in Chapter 6.

(iv) Initially it will be assumed that there is no government activity. This is introduced later in this chapter.

GROSS NATIONAL PRODUCT

Now broadly, G.N.P. measures the output of goods and services at market prices. It is widely considered to be the best available

[1] Some writers draw diagrams similar to those to be developed here, exhibiting a trade-off between *growth* and pollution. Their interpretation is obscure.

measure of the contribution of the 'economic system' to human welfare. This claim may be illustrated by Fig. 1. Though the type of diagram will probably be all too familiar to most readers, it will be worth explaining in some detail, as considerable use will be made of similar diagrams in the course of this book.

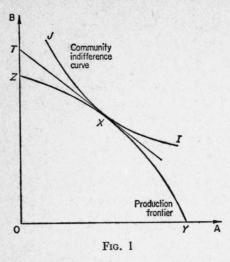

Fig. 1

Fig. 1 exhibits output combinations of two ordinary marketed goods, A and B, supposedly the only two goods produced. The area $0YZ$ represents the set of attainable combinations which can be produced. If individuals are 'rational' (successful maximisers of their own welfare) and if markets are perfect (no monopolies, no externalities, etc.) an optimal position X will be reached, at which the slope of the tangent (XT) is equal to the price ratio P_B/P_A. G.N.P. (in terms of B-goods) is $0T$ and, given the price ratio, this is clearly the maximum value attainable.

The figure illustrates the claim of (perfect) markets to guide the economy to an optimum position and the claim of G.N.P. to be a measure of welfare. It will be seen that both claims depend on prices providing correct measures of marginal values and both are, to a greater or lesser extent, invalidated by irrationality or market failure.

Anti-growth men (and others) have attacked the relative valuations of the market. In particular, the assumption of consumer rationality is widely questioned [28, 98]. However, as this book is concerned with the conflict between marketed goods and environmental services, we shall, for convenience, accept G.N.P. as a valid measure of the (direct) contribution of the former to welfare (see [24]).

ENVIRONMENTAL SERVICES

The most serious deficiency of G.N.P. as a welfare measure, however, is its limited coverage. Apart from public expenditure (discussed below), it includes only those goods and services which are sold on the market.[1] However, not even economists suppose that these are the only or necessarily the major determinants of welfare. Individual welfare depends also on services which cannot be, or at least generally are not, bought or sold. It depends, for example, on the quality of the air around us, of the water we bathe or fish in, of the landscape and the townscape and the sounds that assail our ears at every turn. Together these may be termed *the physical environment*. It depends also on social factors, personal relationships with family, friends, neighbours, colleagues at work or casual acquaintances, and on such things as vandalism and crime. These may be termed *the social environment*.

The distinction between the social and the physical environment is not entirely clear cut. For our purposes this does not matter, since we are concerned with conflicts between G.N.P. and the environment, physical and social. We shall have physical phenomena mainly in mind, because these are better understood and much easier to relate to economic variables; but in principle the analysis is equally applicable to social phenomena.

The term 'environment' is variously used to denote a *stock* and a *flow*. The stock concept relates to, for example, the

[1] The national-income accountant generally imputes values to certain non-marketed items with close marketed substitutes, notably food consumed by producers (a very important item in poor countries) and hypothetical rent on owner-occupied dwellings. In principle, imputation procedures may be extended to environmental phenomena. An attempt to do this is discussed in the Appendix.

quality of the water, while the flow concept relates to the stream of satisfactions which the stock provides. Somewhat analogously, the stock of machines yields a flow of marketed goods and services (which we shall call M-goods). To avoid confusion we shall use *Environmental Capital* to refer to the stock concept, *Environment Services* (or E-goods) to refer to the flow concept. This chapter and the next centre round conflicts between M-goods and E-goods.

The stock concept is also used more widely to embrace certain classes of productive capital, in particular *natural resources*. Resource depletion is often referred to as an environmental problem. This problem however raises rather different issues and discussion is deferred until Chapter 4.

PUBLIC GOODS AND EXTERNALITIES

The 'environmental' problems we shall be looking at stem from two related sources of market failure. The first is that some goods, known as 'public goods', have properties which inhibit their sale on markets (e.g. defence). Such goods are characterised by non-rivalness (that is, I can consume the good without affecting your consumption of it) and non-excludability (if the goods are provided at all, they cannot but be provided for everybody). Under these circumstances, pricing is socially pointless and anyway impossible; the goods are therefore provided free or not at all. Both non-rivalness and non-excludability are matters of degree and are not necessarily correlated; also the group to which the goods are 'public' range from the nation or even the world to a small group sharing, say, a water pipe. Few goods are pure public goods, but a wide range of goods have public goods characteristics which make provision by the market, to a greater or lesser extent, unsatisfactory. (See [106]).

The second source of market failure is that some activities involve externalities, that is side effects on other people in respect of which no payment is made. These effects may be favourable, as when a firm erects a beautiful building which gives pleasure to passers-by, or (more commonly) unfavourable, as when a firm erects an ugly one or a householder uses his noisy lawnmower. Unless the government intervenes, the individual

16

or firm has no incentive (except, hopefully, altruism) to take the externality into account. Externalities may affect one or many. If many, the public-good terminology becomes appropriate. River quality, for example, may be seen as a public good (provided by nature) which pollution degrades. Alternatively, river pollution may be described as a public bad.

The environment may thus be viewed as a collection of goods, mostly public, such as air quality, water quality, visual beauty, space and so on. The activities of man will affect the environment for good or ill. Some of these activities, particularly by the government and certain charitable institutions, may have the public interest in mind. However most activities are more narrowly conceived in terms of individual interests. Because of external effects, such activities frequently degrade the environment, while the difficulties associated with financing public goods mean that many opportunities for improving the environment are missed.

MARKET FAILURE AND G.N.P.

Some externalities impinge on producers. For example, a factory may incur costs in purifying polluted river water or in delays to its lorries caused by road congestion. Such externalities affect welfare – not directly, but through losses in producer efficiency. Evaluation of the costs of these externalities in monetary terms is comparatively straightforward. Such distortions cause production to take place *inside* the production frontier (YXZ in Fig. 1); G.N.P. falls, and even a G.N.P.-maximising government will wish to eliminate such externalities. There is thus no conflict between G.N.P. and environment in this case. For what might be termed 'the producer environment' is fully reflected in G.N.P., at least in the static case. These externalities will henceforth be ignored.

Other externalities impinge directly on consumers, as for example when river pollution affects bathing.[1] Bathing is a free good, and a deterioration in its quality is in no way reflected in

[1] Except where the river is privately owned and bathing facilities provided commercially. The classification of externalities is thus dependent on institutions.

17

G.N.P. Production of marketed goods is not affected, and production occurs on the production boundary YZ. The only trouble now is that this diagram no longer tells the whole story since certain goods (river bathing) do not figure in it.

The externality framework is applicable to a wide variety of phenomena. Social critics may complain of the impact of gun sales on the murder rate, or of television sets on cultural life. In both cases, it is being alleged that A's purchase has non-marketed effects on other members of the community. Similarly if, as Duesenberry alleged [83], welfare is a function of relative rather than absolute consumptions, then one man's consumption has adverse external effects on his neighbour's welfare. A Galbraithian [98] expansion of wants through advertising constitutes a producer–consumer externality. While it may be stretching terminology to describe all these as environmental effects, they may be regarded as examples of the analysis here presented. In any case they result in systematic distortions of G.N.P. as a welfare measure.

Earlier, E-goods and E-bads were equated with public goods and bads. This suggests a direct role for the government in the provision of public goods and the alleviation of public bads (e.g. litter collection, sewage treatment, police, defence). Such expenditure is designed to improve the quality of the environment, in the wide sense in which we have defined it. The value of such expenditure is a measure (though not a very good one) of the value of the environmental improvement. Such expenditure, which is of course included in G.N.P., should be classified as E-goods rather than M-goods output.[1] This serves to break the simple link between M-goods and G.N.P.

THE STATIC CONFLICT

Now let us consider, in its simplest form, the conflict between the generation of M-goods and E-goods. Fig. 2 illustrates the possibilities. At one extreme, all resources can be devoted to

[1] Whether all government expenditure should be so classified is arguable. Consider, for example, health, which though provided publicly in the United Kingdom could be provided privately and indeed is in many countries.

18

producing M-goods, at whatever environmental cost; the economy then operates at Z. Reductions in environmental damage may be achieved either by modifying production methods, or by devoting some resources to projects for environmental improvement. At the other extreme X, no M-goods are produced, all resources being devoted to maintaining a high quality environment. Between these extremes lies a continuous spectrum of alternatives.

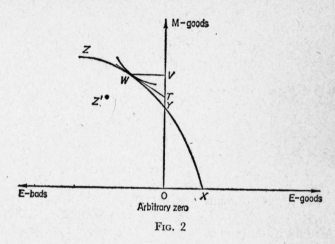

Fig. 2

If no provision is made for externalities or public goods, the economy will operate at Z.[1] This is also the consequence of G.N.P. maximisation. In general, one would expect neither Z nor the opposite extreme X to be optimal. The optimum is likely to be some intermediate position, say W, depending on social preferences.

In principle, the method of deriving G.N.P. may be extended to embrace the value of environmental quality so as to give a 'corrected' or 'generalised' measure. At W, the ratio of the marginal utility of environmental quality to the marginal utility or production of conventional goods is given by the slope of the tangent WT. Now define a zero for environmental

[1] In as far as externalities affect producers (see p. 17) the economy will move to a position within the frontier, say Z' (which may be either to the right or the left of Z).

19

quality – arbitrarily, for in contrast to M-goods production there is no obvious or natural zero. $0T$ (rather than $0V$) provides a generalised welfare measure. Given the relative valuation associated with W, generalised G.N.P. is maximised at this point.

A COMPARATIVE STATIC MODEL

Now consider what happens as production possibilities expand through time. Such an expansion is initially conceived as 'dropping like manna from heaven', e.g. through effortless advances in knowledge. Possible connections between choices in the first period and possibilities in the second period, such as might arise through investment, research, persistent pollution or resource depletion are ruled out (until the next chapter). Fig. 3 shows the result.

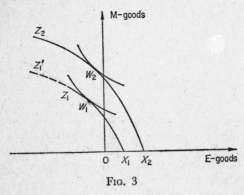

Fig. 3

At worst, technical advance simply expands the possibilities for production of M-goods beyond X_1Z_1 to Z_1'. If optimal output previously lay to the right of Z_1 it will be unaffected by such a shift. If at Z_1, however, it may shift leftwards to a point on Z_1Z_1', and environmental quality may fall. If E-goods are unpriced, production will move from Z_1 to Z_1'; environmental quality, and quite possibly welfare, may decline. This is a very simple example of a case of advancing knowledge and the resulting expansion of possibilities leading to a decline in welfare (cf. [19]).

20

Hopefully, technical advance involves a shift in the whole schedule upwards to X_2Z_2 in Fig. 3. Optimally, welfare increases. There is some expectation that both material product and environmental quality will improve, as in the shift $W_1 \rightarrow W_2$ illustrated.

However this outcome is by no means certain. All depends on the shape of (and movements in) the community preference map and on the shift in the production possibility frontier. Fig. 4 shows two special cases.

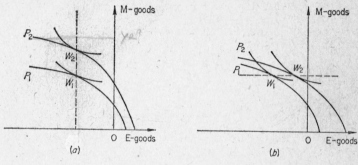

FIG. 4

In the first, $4(a)$, the common marginal rates of transformation and substitution (M.R.T. and M.R.S.) are constant at a constant standard of environmental quality; in the second, $4(b)$, they are constant at a constant level of material output. In the first case material output expands with environmental quality constant; in the second, environmental quality improves with material output constant. A complete taxonomy is given in Table 1 (p. 22). The shift on the demand side is defined in terms of the normal concept of inferiority. An analogous classification is employed on the supply side in terms of the point Y_2 at which P_2 has the same slope as P_1 has at W_1. If Y_2 lies to the *left* of W_1, the shift is said to be strongly biased towards M-goods, if *below* W_1, towards E-goods; otherwise it is said to be intermediate. It will be seen that in no case can we be certain about the direction of movement of all three variables.

These are all shifts between optimal positions. If, at the opposite extreme, *no* allowance is made for environmental effects, the effect may be quite different – e.g. Z_1 to Z_2 in Fig. 3. Such a shift involves an increase in material production but quite possibly a decline in environmental quality and even in welfare. These possibilities are quite consistent with the *optimal* movement involving an improvement in environmental quality.

TABLE 1

The Effect of an Expansion in Output on E, M, M.R.T.

Supply side \ Demand side	E-goods inferior	Both goods normal	M-goods inferior
Strongly biased towards M-goods	E↓ M↑ M.R.T.?	E? M↑ M.R.T.↓	E? M? M.R.T.↓
Intermediate	E? M↑ M.R.T.↓	E↓ M↑ M.R.T.?	E↓ M? M.R.T.↓
Strongly biased towards E-goods	E? M? M.R.T.↓	E↓ M? M.R.T.↓	E↓ M↑ M.R.T.?

In conclusion, the reader is invited to apply the above framework, to analyse two commonly held views. The first, a popular view, is exemplified by Jacoby and Pennance's [22] contention that 'a rising G.N.P. will enable a nation more easily to bear the costs of eliminating pollution'. (Assume, charitably, that the rise in G.N.P. is exogenous, and consider whether pollution levels will, or should, be lower at the higher level of G.N.P.) The second is that, in conditions of poverty, such as exist in the Third World, little importance should be attached to a 'luxury' like environmental quality [47, 52]. (Try to interpret the terms 'importance' and 'luxury' in terms of Fig. 3, and compare the optimal points W_1 and W_2.)

NUMERICAL APPLICATIONS

Nijkamp and Paelinck [38] apply a very similar framework to analyse revealed social preference in the Netherlands. Quantification is achieved by replacing environmental quality by environmental expenditure on the horizontal axis, as in Fig. 5. This allows zero to be defined in the normal way so that the normal definitions of elasticities, luxuries and necessities can be applied. Since 1963, environmental expenditure in the Netherlands has risen over twice as fast as the rest of G.N.P.; this is explained in terms of the shape of the preference map which is 'bunched' to the right. Not only is environmental quality a luxury, but proportionately more environmental expenditure is needed to combat the increasingly severe effects of other expenditure on the environment as certain biological and psychological limits are approached. This key interdependence on the production side remains implicit.

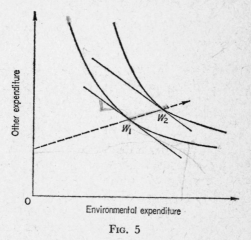

Fig. 5

The model is chiefly interesting for the attempt to attain precision through measurement. This is, however, achieved at considerable cost, in that environmental expenditure, if it is to be measurable, must be very narrowly and arbitrarily defined and, thus defined, is but one among many ways of enhancing, or preventing the deterioration of, the environment.

In fact Nijkamp and Paelinck's measure comprises various categories of government expenditure. The authors recognise that in principle the list could be extended to include expenditure by private firms on, for example, anti-pollution devices, although at present such statistics are not generally collected.

23

But should it not also include any change in production methods or in the mix of goods produced due to environmental taxes or regulations or otherwise on environmental grounds? A broad definition of environmental expenditure would be in terms of opportunity cost, the value of material goods forgone. Zero environmental quality would then be the level corresponding to maximal material output. Such a definition, which would leave Nijkamp and Paelinck's theoretical discussion intact, would however pose virtually insuperable measurement problems. It is important too to note that even a broad concept of environmental expenditure does not correspond to our concept of environmental quality. In particular, as production possibilities expand, zero environmental expenditure will represent a deteriorating level of environmental quality.

There is some evidence that advanced economies may be operating on a rather flat portion of the curve, that is that 'substantial' improvements in environmental quality could be achieved at low cost. Kneese [23] estimates the cost of achieving substantial reductions in environmental pollution in the United States at $95 billion. This amounts to nearly 10 per cent of G.N.P. but, since much of this expenditure, including the costly separation of storm from sanitary sewers, is of a once-and-for-all nature, the *annual* cost would be considerably lower. Such figures of course depend entirely on what is deemed to constitute a 'substantial' improvement.

3 Intertemporal Choice

PRESENT AND FUTURE CONSUMPTION

So far the analysis has been entirely static. Expansion in production opportunities has been introduced, but only as an exogenous element. Expansion of this sort is necessarily potentially beneficial, although we saw that the actual and the potential might well diverge.

Growth theorists have long been concerned with the *deliberate* expansion of future productive opportunities by present investment. Given present production possibilities, this entails a cutback in present consumption. We may thus speak of a trade-off between future output (or growth) and present consumption. However, since output is desired not for its own sake, but because it generates consumption, it is more illuminating to look at the trade-off between future consumption and present consumption. The basic idea may be illustrated in the familiar neo-classical diagram shown in Fig. 6.

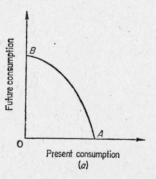
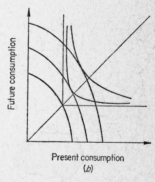

FIG. 6

For simplicity, suppose a fixed group of individuals face a choice between consumption in just two periods, the 'present' and the 'future'. The set of feasible combinations (the area $0AB$)

25

is determined by production possibilities. In general, it is to be expected that $0B > 0A$ due to technical advance and the advantages of 'round-about' (i.e. capital-intensive) production. Once again, with the usual qualifications about income distribution, a perfect market combined with perfect rationality produces the optimum allocation of resources between present and future consumption. The slope of the tangent at the optimal point will be $(1+i)$, where i is the interest rate. At the optimum, i will equal both the marginal rate of substitution (M.R.S.) between present and future consumption (the marginal rate of time preference) and the marginal rate of transformation (M.R.T.).

The position of the optimum will depend on the shape of the preference map. In the absence of 'pure time preference' (generally considered irrational [107, 111]), this will be symmetrical about a 45° line.[1] It follows immediately that, optimally, future consumption will exceed (or, in the limiting case, equal) present consumption. Also, near subsistence levels of consumption, the preference map is presumably almost rectangular, but as consumption rises the curvature falls; correspondingly the optimum point tends to diverge increasingly from the 45° line. Little else can be said in general about the optimum point.

In practice of course, the optimum will not be attained, be-

---

[1] The reader is reminded of the simplifying assumption of a fixed population. Allowing for the succession of generations provides a further reason for pure time preference, which will now occur unless the present generation gives equal weight to its own and to its successors' welfare. Such pure time preference may still be considered as morally wrong and regarded as a bias in the market mechanism for intertemporal allocation (see p. 78). If the population is growing, the diagram may be redrawn in terms of consumption per head and pure time preference redefined accordingly. The shape of the feasibility set is however not then altogether clear and it is not obvious whether, optimally, consumption per head rises or falls through time. Finally, if population growth is endogenous, a function of present consumption, the analysis is complicated enormously [101]. Apart from a brief discussion in the context of resource depletion (p. 47), complications arising from endogenous demographic change will be ignored throughout the book.

cause of market imperfections and irrationality. In an interesting paper [34] Tobin considers various sources of market imperfection affecting the M.R.S. and the M.R.T. which of themselves constitute a bias against future consumption and hence a justification for government intervention to raise the growth rate. They are myopia, neglect of future generations (see footnote, p. 26), monopolistic elements in capital markets, excessive risk aversion associated with inadequate risk-pooling institutions, and certain externalities associated with investment, especially in research and development and human capital. We shall not stop to examine Tobin's arguments as they do not concern environmental issues (see however [24, 31]). What is chiefly interesting here is Tobin's method; for many environmentalists argue, contrary to Tobin, that the growth rate should be reduced. It is interesting to see how far their arguments can be developed in terms of Tobin's model.

INTRODUCING ENVIRONMENTAL ISSUES

Tobin was concerned with intertemporal choice. Writing before the environmental furore, he accepted uncritically the conventional measure of consumption as an indicator of welfare. With one exception (leisure), he did not consider the possibility that there might be other components of welfare (environmental services) of which the conventional measures take no account.

We shall consider three ways of introducing environmental issues. The first sticks closest to the letter of the original model, employing conventional definitions of consumption and investment; E-goods appear as externalities which serve to modify or even reverse the link between consumption (including the concomitant production and investment) and welfare. The second (which Tobin would undoubtedly have preferred) involves a broadening of the definition of consumption and output to include E-goods and of investment to refer to an extension of the capacity of the economy to produce output as freshly defined. The third involves distinguishing M-goods and E-goods separately.

27

AN EXTERNALITIES APPROACH

Tobin argued that investment yields future benefits not perceived by decision-makers. However it may also yield a variety of future disbenefits.

Many investments, especially land-intensive investments, involve, in the first instance, a destruction of environmental services such as scenic beauty. In as far as there is *ex post* substitution between M-goods and E-goods, future decision-makers may seek to offset the effect on the environment, but this they can only do at the expense of M-goods output thereby reducing the benefits of the investment. In terms of Fig. 3, the investment may be seen as pushing the production possibility frontier simultaneously to the north (the production effect) and to the west (the environmental effect). The latter may indeed dominate so that production possibilities actually contract. (Even if the curve expands, this is no guarantee that the *actual* movement will be a beneficial one – see p. 20.) In any case, the investors will tend to take account only of the favourable production effect and not of the unfavourable environmental effect. It is clear that this constitutes a bias similar in type but opposite in direction to those considered by Tobin.

A similar effect arises from the additional production ensuing from the investment. This may involve pollution, congestion or noise. In an extreme case these could outweigh the production benefits at the most profitable, or even at *any*, level of production. In the last case, the optimum *ex post* strategy will be to leave the new equipment idle. In the absence of specific measures for environmental protection, the firm will operate the plant at the private optimum, so that social benefits from production will be negative. Even where the net *social* benefits are positive they may not be sufficiently high to outweigh the costs of the investment. In short, there are externalities in the operation of the plant not taken into account by the decision-maker.

Finally, there are externalities connected with consumption. The effect of these is less clear, since the increase in future consumption is offset by a fall in present consumption. The direction of bias may be shown to depend on the movement through time of the marginal rate of substitution between environmental

28

services and material goods [24, 25]. In so far as economic and demographic growth lead to increasing scarcity of the former and increasing abundance of the latter this rate rises leading to an 'anti-Tobin' bias.

It is worth noting that these biases can occur even if society places *no* value on environmental services. For example, road use impinges *inter alia* on commercial vehicles, overfishing depletes fish stocks, water and air pollution impair health and hence labour productivity, pesticide use kills natural predators not only for the farmer concerned but for others.

A GENERALISED MEASURE OF CONSUMPTION

Tobin assumed consumption to be a measure of welfare and G.N.P. of potential welfare. These assumptions are invalidated *inter alia* by environmental phenomena. Since the production of M-goods involves, quite systematically as a by-product, the production of E-bads, the traditional measures are not merely inaccurate but biased. An appealingly direct approach to this problem is to extend the concepts of G.N.P., consumption and investment to include environmental influences on welfare.

The market values M-goods at what individuals are prepared to pay at the margin. These valuations are incorporated in G.N.P. The willingness-to-pay criterion may be used to impute values to goods and services which are not marketed. This principle is of course central to cost–benefit analysis. It is already used by national income accountants in imputing values for food consumed on farms (and the whole subsistence sector in developing countries) and rents of owner-occupied dwellings. Tobin, while making no reference to the environment, proposed making this kind of imputation for the value of leisure. In a later paper with Nordhaus [30], he attempts the imputation of environmental values. The success of this exercise is examined in the Appendix.

The principle involved in imputing values for E-goods is simply illustrated in Fig. 7 (p. 30). If the economy is at X, the relative value of E-goods is given by the tangent to the indifference curve ($I\mathcal{J}$), $X\mathcal{Z}$ (in an optimal position, $X\mathcal{Z}$ will also be a tangent to the production possibility frontier P). Therefore $Y\mathcal{Z}$ is a

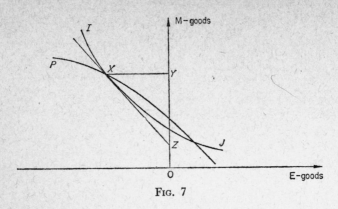

FIG. 7

measure of the disutility of E-bads. The extended consumption
measure is thus $0Y - YZ = 0Z$.

Conventional measures of investment are even more seriously
deficient. Fundamentally, the concept of investment relates to
the deployment of *current* resources to satisfying *future* consumption. But attention is focused almost exclusively on the
installation of man-made capital; this is the major investment
component of G.N.P. It is a commonplace that national product
is more appropriately measured *net* – net of depreciation.
Characteristically, economists prefer the *gross* concept, because,
however unsuitable it may be to their needs, they can measure
it with greater accuracy. Labour training, education, health,
research and development have an important investment component, but are generally classified as consumption or intermediate expenditure; in the latter case they are omitted from
national product altogether.

More relevant to our theme, national product omits such items
as resource depletion, persistent pollution, emergence of new
pests, extinction of species, and deterioration of landscape.[1]

[1] The list could indeed be extended to include changes in the
social environment, such as the severance of communities by motor-
ways, the breakdown of traditional living patterns by rehousing,
increases in stress, vandalism and crime. These could be viewed as
disinvestment affecting welfare both directly and indirectly via
adverse effects on production. A Galbraithian increase in wants
could, because of its adverse effect on welfare, also be viewed as
disinvestment.

30

These the economist ignores, again largely because he finds them so hard to measure. This is legitimate only if either they are quantitatively unimportant (as Nordhaus and Tobin suggest is the case with resource depletion – see Chapter 4) or if they are independent of economic activity.

Having redefined consumption and investment and hence 'output', let us return to Tobin's analysis. Tobin assumed points on his frontier to represent maximum levels of future welfare for given levels of current welfare. In so far as Tobin ignored an important component of welfare, namely E-goods, this assumption was suspect. We have now redefined consumption more broadly to include E-goods and hence to validate the original assumption.

Tobin was concerned with selection between frontier points. Imperfections related to investment as a whole and to production or consumption as a whole (e.g. myopia, neglect of future generations) will move the economy round the intertemporal frontier from the optimal point to a sub-optimal one.

In fact, his analysis was never entirely satisfactory, in that many of the distortions discussed were more or less specific to particular types of investment. Inappropriate attention to risk, monopoly in capital markets and learning-by-doing effects unquestionably vary widely between sectors. Labour-training and research-and-development externalities are definitionally related to specific forms of investment activity. Such imperfections move the economy not round but *inside* the frontier. Future consumption may be increased simply by altering the pattern of investment (e.g. in favour of research and development), while leaving total investment and hence present consumption unchanged. A policy of increasing investment in general will have too little impact on research and development compared with its impact on other sorts of investment and will move the economy from one interior position to another, possibly superior, possibly not.

We have introduced a number of environmental imperfections. These are basically of two types (i) those which impinge on firms and hence classify as externalities even if no value is put on E-goods; and (ii) those which impinge on consumers directly and are of significance only if E-goods are valued. Type (i)

31

imperfections are similar in type though opposite in direction to those considered by Tobin. In so far as they are independent of the mix of investment, production or consumption, they move the economy round the frontier. In fact, congestion, pollution, resource depletion, etc., vary widely between sectors. Type (ii) imperfections definitionally distort the balance between M-goods and E-goods. Clearly,[1] future (present) welfare may be increased by altering the *composition* of future (present) consumption in favour of E-goods, leaving present (future) consumption unchanged. In other words environmental distortions necessarily place the economy inside the frontier.

For the moment, suppose these last varieties of imperfections to be the only ones in an otherwise perfect market. They do not constitute a distortion in the mechanism for intertemporal choice, and remedies conceived in terms of the generalised growth rate (using the extended definitions of consumption and output) do not seem appropriate. The environmentalists' attack, however, is not on the generalised growth rate, but on the growth rate *as it is currently measured*. The arguments of the last sections indicated that a reduction of measured growth would be likely to benefit the environment. Nevertheless to attack a distortion between M-goods and E-goods by altering the balance between present and future M-goods consumption seems a somewhat indirect and inefficient approach to the problem!

Much of the confusion in the literature indeed stems from a failure to distinguish with sufficient clarity the trade-off between present and future on the one hand and between M-goods and E-goods on the other. Accordingly in the next section we introduce a model which makes this distinction explicit.

[1] Unless M-goods and E-bads are strictly joint products, not only commodity by commodity, but for any mix of M-goods consumption. Such an assumption is in fact implicit in some of the anti-growth literature. There have also been models constructed which embody the opposite assumption of a fixed savings ratio and explore the consequences of different combinations of productive and environmental investment [35, 36].

A 2 (GOODS) × 2 (TIME PERIODS) MODEL

The static model of Chapter 2 is here combined with the intertemporal model to yield a model with four goods: (i) present M-goods; (ii) present E-goods; (iii) future M-goods; and (iv) future E-goods.

The model cannot be represented diagrammatically, but it is clear (and simply proved algebraically) that optimality entails equality between the M.R.S. and the M.R.T. for each pair of goods, a sufficient condition of which is that both equal the corresponding relative prices. There are in fact three independent price ratios, from which the other three may be derived. Of these, four are of particular interest:

(1) the relative price of M-goods and E-goods in the present (the slope of the production frontier in Fig. 2) (P_1);

(2) the same price relative in the future (P_2);

(3) the relative price of present M-goods and future M-goods $(1+i)$; and

(4) the relative price of present E-goods and future E-goods $(1+j)$.

This last, which may be termed the 'own-interest rate' of environmental quality, is related to the other three by the formula

$$(1+j) = (1+i) \, P_2/P_1 \tag{1}$$

To reach the optimum, the government clearly needs three policies corresponding to the three independent sets of prices:

(1) a policy for encouraging current environmental services;

(2) a policy for encouraging future environmental services; and

(3) a policy towards intertemporal choice (this may be conceived purely in terms of material goods. Intertemporal balance in terms of environmental services is then automatically ensured by equation (1)).

Environmentalists are often accused of attempting to control environmental quality via policies related to the (measured) growth rate (e.g. [21]). From this model it is clear that, in general, three policies are required to achieve the optimum and use of one policy instrument only constitutes a second-best approach where the constraints on the other marginal rates are, quite unnecessarily, accepted as given. Nevertheless, were these constraints truly binding, a growth-reducing policy might well be the best then available and in any case constitute an improvement on *laissez-faire*.

In fact the position of environmentalists on this issue is often unclear and probably not uniform. Some writers argue rather vaguely for a reduction in the growth rate, without seeming to realise that alternative means of environmental control exist which might render a general growth-reducing policy unnecessary. Other writers, for example Mishan [28], while attacking growth, recommend highly specific policies for environmental control, which correspond in our general model to controls P_1 and P_2. Such policies, if carried out with the vigour which Mishan recommends, would no doubt reduce measured growth, as he is doubtless well aware. But that is another matter. A third group of writers present more sophisticated argument for halting economic growth. These will be considered in Chapter 5.

Finally, this model may be used to illuminate an environmentalist's dilemma over the discount rate. For, according to the traditional (Tobin) model, greater weight is given to the interests of future generations by *lowering* the discount rate. Indeed, some environmentalists object to any discounting of the future especially in relation to environmental items like noise. On the other hand, the practical effect of lowering the discount rate is to raise investment and hence (measured) growth to the detriment of future generations.

The point is of course that it is not measured growth *per se* that the environmentalists are objecting to, but its concomitant environmental ill-effects. If this link cannot be broken, then the growth rate must be lowered and this implies raising the discount rate.[1] In this context the conventional presumption that a lower discount rate favours the future is not valid. However such an approach is, as we saw, second best.

If direct environmental policies are available, then these, rather than the discount rate, may be used to protect both the

[1] See also the discussion of the discount rate in the context of resource depletion (p. 50).

34

future and the present environment. In so far as the link between M-goods production and adverse environmental effects is broken, the rationale for anti-growth policies (such as a high discount rate) is weakened.

Finally notice that E-goods have their own discount rate (j). Discounting M-goods does not necessarily imply discounting E-goods. If the relative marginal value of E-goods increases over time $(P_1 > P_2)$ as is generally accepted to be the case with, for example, noise, then from equation (1) $j < i$. Specifically, if the relative marginal value of E-goods increases by 10 per cent between the two time periods, the $j = i - 10$ per cent; if $i = 10$ per cent, $j = 0$. Even negative values of j are not necessarily inconsistent with a conventional 10 per cent for i.

4 Resource Depletion

So far it has been assumed that, through capital accumulation and technical progress, growth can continue indefinitely, though maybe at the expense of environmental amenity. Growth today provides, as it were, a spring-board for growth tomorrow. But G.N.P. is produced not only with man-made capital which can be augmented, but with natural resources, which cannot.[1] Indeed, present levels of production are *using up* natural resources at a rate which alarms resource pessimists; fossil fuels are burnt and lands overworked, leaving our descendants with smaller fuel stocks and degraded land. 'Present reserves of all but a few metals will be exhausted within fifty years if consumption rates continue to grow as they are' and more generally 'if current trends are allowed to persist . . . the breakdown of society and the irreversible disruption of the life support systems on this planet are inevitable' [46].

Resource optimists reject this gloomy scenario: 'There are no substantial limits in sight either in raw materials or in energy that the price structure, product substitution, anticipated gains in technology and pollution control cannot be expected to solve' [103]. Nordhaus and Tobin [30] go further: they can find no evidence that 'natural resources [will] become an increasingly severe drag on economic growth. Indeed the opposite seems likely: growth of output per capita will accelerate ever so slightly even as stocks of natural resources decline'. Kay and Mirrlees [62] even suggest that 'there is a real danger that the world's resources are being used too slowly. . . . In general we believe that the interests of future generations will be better served if we leave them production equipment rather than minerals in the ground.'

[1] Of course it is generally agreed that output ought, in principle, to be measured *net* – net of depreciation and resource depletion. The possibilities are considered in the Appendix. In this chapter growth is conceived, in the usual way, in terms of G.N.P.

TYPES OF RESOURCES

Resources are customarily divided into 'renewable' and 'non-renewable'. Non-renewable resources cannot be used without depletion; fossil fuels provide the paradigm. Total stocks are, for all practical purposes, fixed, thus setting a limit on cumulative use.

Other resources, such as agricultural land and fisheries, can yield output indefinitely without impairing their productivity and are said to be renewable. Renewal is not however automatic: such resources may be depleted, perhaps totally and irreversibly by heavy use (overcropping or overfishing) or misuse. Maximum production consistent with maintaining future productivity is known as maximum sustainable yield (M.S.Y.). Stocks of renewable resources may also be augmented by investment[1] or sometimes by mere abstention, as when overworked land is allowed to recover its fertility. But these are possibilities which we shall, for the time being, set aside.

Mineral resources are generally classified as non-renewable. Yet, while they can be mined only once, they are dissipated rather than destroyed by production and thus are, in principle at least, available for recycling. Thus, ultimately, recycling possibilities set a limit on *sustainable* use and such resources are, in this sense, renewable. Such limits may however be very low in relation to current extraction from mines.

LIMITS TO GROWTH: A RENEWABLE RESOURCE

Our strategy will be to set out some very simple models. These are designed to highlight particular issues and to illustrate characteristic modes of thought. Complications will be introduced one at a time.

Suppose first that there is a single consumer good (say food) produced from a single renewable resource (land). Population and M.S.Y. per acre are both fixed. However land in cultiva-

[1] Many of these methods are however controversial. Practices, such as pesticide spraying and use of inorganic fertilisers, which bring about substantial medium-term increases in yield, carry long-term dangers (p. 43).

tion grows exponentially through time and, with it, the production of food.

Eventually the physical limits are reached. No more land can be cleared without seriously impairing the productivity of land already in cultivation. (This is an entirely realistic assumption: excessive land clearance often reduces rainfall and protection from wind, besides initiating ecological changes.) The economy has reached the point *C* in Fig. 8. In theory, of course, growth

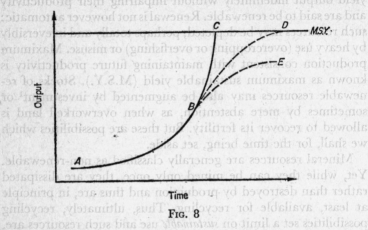

FIG. 8

could be halted at this point and M.S.Y. sustained thereafter – indeed this appears an attractive strategy. In practice, however, this is likely to be difficult.

First, notice that the limit is approached with surprising rapidity. Suppose, for example, production grows at the comparatively modest rate of 3 per cent per annum: this implies a doubling every 23 years and a twenty-fold increase every 100 years. Thus in a mere 23 years, a situation of abundance with half the land unused is transferred into one of scarcity. Secondly, at *C*, people will be accustomed to a rising standard of living and will attempt to maintain the improvement. Controls over land clearance will probably be less than perfectly effective. There will be people who dispute that further land clearance is damaging to M.S.Y., and special claims will no doubt be made for the poor (cf. Chapter 6). It is probable that land clearance will continue, as well as overcropping of existing land. A society

38

wishing to avoid such an outcome would be wise to anticipate the limits, slowing off growth at say *B* and attempting to follow the path *ABD*, or better *ABE* to allow a margin for error. Some resource optimists (e.g. [21, 52]) emphasise that growth is difficult to stop. However this only increases the importance of beginning in good time.

This kind of model will be recognised as 'Malthusian' although it is somewhat of a caricature of Malthus's views. Similar models are set out in the expositional chapters of Meadows's notorious *Limits to Growth* [49], although Meadows's model itself is more sophisticated (see [50–5, 62, 63]).

LIMITS TO GROWTH: A NON-RENEWABLE RESOURCE

Suppose, instead, production to be from a non-renewable resource. Suppose, as before, resource productivity and population to be fixed. The stock now places a limit on *cumulative* production from the resource. Under exponential growth, exhaustion will be rapid in the later stages, as Fig. 9 illustrates.

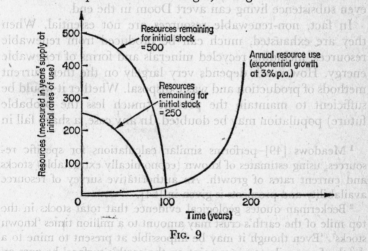

FIG. 9

Known reserves are generally expressed in terms of years' supply at current rates of use. However usage of most resources is growing rapidly, and this naturally hastens the exhaustion date. For example at 3 per cent per annum growth, 250 years' mineral supply lasts about 80 years.[1]

Resource optimists point out that *known* resources are a reflection more of mining companies' search policies than of *total* resources – that, as known stocks are used up, the companies will seek out new deposits to keep the known stock/usage rates approximately constant [50]. There is some truth in this, but limited comfort. Current figures for known stocks may be consistent with abundance; they are consistent also with impending exhaustion. In fact, as less and less of the world remains unsearched, the possibilities of discovering new resources diminishes [64]. Also it should be emphasised that, in the face of exponential growth in demands, quite large new discoveries make surprisingly little difference to the date of exhaustion. Fig. 9 illustrates how a doubling of supplies delays the date by a mere 25 years.[2]

But even at constant rates of use, exhaustible resources are eventually exhausted. Even the Doom-averting final run of the *Limits to Growth* model involves a rapid rate of resource depletion and total exhaustion in the twenty-fourth century. If these resources are essential to production and human life, then not even subsistence living can avert Doom in the end.

In fact, non-renewable resources are not essential. When they are exhausted, much can be produced from renewable resources, including recycled minerals and forms of renewable energy. How much depends very largely on the then current methods of production and waste disposal. Whether it would be sufficient to maintain the present (much less the probable future) population may be doubted. In any case, a sharp fall in

[1] Meadows [49] performs similar calculations for specific resources, using estimates of known (economically extractable) stocks and current rates of growth. An authoritative survey of resource availability and prospects is given in [64].

[2] Beckerman quotes geological evidence that total stocks in the top mile of the earth's crust may amount to a million times 'known stocks'. 'Even though it may be impossible at present to mine to a depth of one mile at every point on the earth's surface' he goes on 'by the year A.D. 100,000,000 I am sure we will think up something.' But at 3 per cent per annum growth rather greater inventiveness is required, for even this is gone in about 500 years!

material living standards would be inevitable and the longer growth persists the sharper this fall would be. The problems of adapting to M.S.Y. encountered in our model of a non-renewable resource reappear in exaggerated form. People are becoming increasingly reliant on generous diets, warm and uniform temperatures and modern medicines and may be unable to survive without them, In short, the experiences of the growth period will have totally unfitted the population for the near-subsistence conditions that follow. These considerations contradict economists' usual assumption of exogenous wants and are therefore generally neglected. Galbraith [98] and others have of course raised the issue but in a different (and less critical) context. Though man's adaptability to adverse circumstances is often asserted, evidence appears to be sparse (but see [97]).

INCREASING RESOURCE PRODUCTIVITY

So far, resource productivity has been assumed constant. As resource optimists emphasise, this is a very unrealistic assumption. There are several ways in which overall resource productivity may be increased:

(1) By changes in the composition of output. Unit resource requirements vary widely between different components of G.N.P. (compare for example a car and a lesson in meditation).

(2) By substitution between factor inputs. Substitution between different resources of the same type is of limited significance, for it affects the magnitude rather than the existence of the ultimate limits; substitution between non-renewable and renewable resources is of more importance, as we saw in the previous section; most important of all is the possibility of substitution between natural resources and man-made capital. For, as natural resources are depleted, man-made capital is accumulated; the increasing abundance of the latter offsets the increasing scarcity of the former, increasing its productivity.

(3) By technical progress.

Now it is easily demonstrated that apparently generous once-for-all increases in resource productivity make very little impact on resource limits. (This is what Meadows means when he claims that his model is insensitive to assumptions about technical progress.) For example, if output is growing at 3 per cent per annum, a twenty-fold increase in resource productivity puts back the limit by approximately 100 years.

However a twenty-fold increase in resource productivity does not sound quite so improbable when re-expressed as a 3 per cent per annum increase in resource productivity maintained over 100 years. Indeed it is obvious that, if resource productivity grows at the same rate as output, the limit recedes indefinitely. Indeed, even if a non-renewable resource is essential to production, growth may proceed unchecked, without the resource ever becoming totally exhausted – provided the increase in resource productivity is fast enough. Suppose output grows at 3 per cent per annum, and resource productivity grows at 6 per cent per annum. Resource use will fall by approximately 3 per cent per annum,[1] and cumulative resource use will have a finite sum equal to thirty-three times resource use in the initial year. If total resource stocks exceed this figure, growth can continue at 3 per cent indefinitely without exhaustion of the resource.

This line of reasoning serves a strictly limited purpose – it disproves the *inevitability* of the *Limits to Growth* scenario. It establishes the *logical conceivability*, not the certainty, probability or even the possibility in practice, of growth continuing indefinitely. Everything hinges on the rate of technical progress and possibilities of substitution. This is perhaps the main issue that separates resource optimists and resource pessimists. The optimist believes in the power of human inventiveness to solve whatever problems are thrown in its way, as apparently it has done in the past. The pessimist questions the success of these past technological solutions and fears that future problems may be more intractable. Let us examine these arguments a little more closely.

Barnett and Morse [56] document numerous historical examples of impending shortages of particular resources, which

[1] While this is conceivable, growth is currently being sustained by rising usage of most resources.

caused serious alarm at the time, but which were averted by substitution or technical change, often as a direct response to the shortage. (See also [47, 52] and for a rather different view of the process [94]).

Barnett and Morse pass to a systematic examination of trends in extraction costs and prices of major resource products over the period from 1860 to 1957. As resources become increasingly scarce, one would expect a rise both in exploitation costs (as inferior-quality resources are pressed into service) and in the relative prices of resource products. Barnett and Morse tested both these implications finding them to be (mostly) contradicted by experience. In all cases, except forestry, exploitation costs exhibited a definite fall, which must be interpreted largely as resulting from improvements in technology in the resource industries concerned; prices exhibited fluctuations about trends that were, if anything, falling, providing a more general indication that resource scarcity was, during the period, overcome by substitution and technology. These findings are, however, disputed, for at least some commodities, by Lovering in [64].

Denison [96] and Nordhaus and Tobin [30] both consider the impact of land and natural resources on economic growth. Denison concludes that resource availability has had a small and declining impact. Nordhaus and Tobin find events most satisfactorily explained by either resource-saving technical change or a high substitutability between natural resources and man-made capital. These conclusions stem from the declining factor shares accruing to owners of natural resources, despite increasing inputs of both capital and labour.

As far as non-renewable resources are concerned, these results are of limited significance, being consistent with the pessimist's worst fears. Technical advances in exploitation simply serve to keep down product prices thus encouraging rapid exploitation rather than economy in use. Short-run scarcity is thereby alleviated, but the exhaustion dates may well be brought forward. For while the size of the economically extractable stock is expanded, so is the rate at which it is extracted.

The implications for renewable resources are more encourag-

43

ing, provided the quality of resources is being maintained.[1] An 'advance' in exploitation technology may involve an increase in M.S.Y. or, if not, may permit a constant yield to be achieved at lower costs, freeing resources for other purposes (exploiting more non-renewable resources?). But they may simply involve more powerful ways of exceeding M.S.Y., i.e. of mining the resource. In the case of fisheries, technical advance has increased catches and (despite stringent regulations) more and more species are suffering serious depletion [57]. In agriculture too, productivity has been increased by techniques which may have damaging long-term effects. Land clearance may generate aridity and erosion, drainage may cause salination, pesticide spraying may generate new pests while wiping out natural predators, and so on. Quite apart from wider environmental effects, all these phenomena may be seen as depleting the land as an agricultural resource [45].

Of course, depletion will affect exploitation costs and resource product prices and so it is allowed for, up to a point, in the studies. But the effect may be expected to build up over time as the resource becomes increasingly scarce. That over the period explored this effect was small enough to be outweighed by technical advance is little guide to the future.

In other ways too, these studies shed little light on the future. Can it be assumed that in any relevant sense, technology will proceed at a constant rate? Problems may get more difficult, problems may arise which defy solution [54]. It may, for example, be possible to increase M.S.Y. up to a certain point, but then more fundamental biological or physical limits intervene [42, 64].

Frequently too, the solution to one problem generates another possibly more difficult one. Pesticides provide a classic example: Initially the pest is controlled, but later emerges in a more virulent form necessitating a more powerful pesticide. Even if we concentrate on agricultural productivity and neglect the

[1] Nordhaus and Tobin's aggregative study relates ostensibly to renewable resources (p. 60) but their optimistic conclusions ignore the concomitant depletion of non-renewable (as well as renewable) resources, of which no explicit account is taken.

44

serious side-effects, the outcome of this escalation of warfare with the insect world is not at all clear. This example illustrates two further points: (i) even the more immediate side-effects are often unknown when the new technology is put into operation; and (ii) some of the effects (e.g. the build up of D.D.T. in food chains) operate with very long lags.

Finally, technology is not a continuous process; a limited number of key advances are crucial to growth – and perhaps to survival. At the moment, for example, a great deal hangs on the discovery of an economic substitute for the rapidly dwindling supplies of fossil fuels. Nuclear fusion (and perhaps solar energy) could provide virtually unlimited energy if they could be developed at reasonable cost. But, if not, the prospects look pretty grim [64]. Examination of the past can provide no clue to the probability of success. The judgement of experts in the field is probably the best guide but, as so often happens, the experts disagree.[1]

The central feature of technical advance is indeed its *uncertainty*. Resource pessimists, and others, emphasise that future generations should not be subjected even to the risk of global catastrophe. Thus Meade [53] writes: 'The disutility of Doom to future generations would be so great that, even if we gave it a low probability and even if we discount future utilities at a high rate, . . . we would be wise to be very prudent in our present actions' (see also [76]).[2]

Resource pessimists generally argue that this risk, is minimised by a policy of conserving natural resources. However this is the case only if increases in resource productivity are exogenous. In fact, resource productivity may be increased by various forms of investment, by research and development and by accumulation of human skills and physical capital. All these forms of investment (most obviously physical capital) require inputs of natural resources. Such uses involve not a simple depletion of resources but a transformation of their form. It is at least con-

[1] Dasgupta and Heal [59] examine how present depletion of fossil fuels should be influenced by the probability of developing nuclear fusion.

[2] Optimists are wont to misconstrue the significance of this argument (e.g. [50], p. 336, [55], p. 1160).

ceivable that such a transformation increases the ability of future generations to avert Doom [56, 62, 30].

This provides an argument for some uses of resources only. Use of resources for consumption[1] or for many forms of investment (e.g. bingo halls) could be of no conceivable help to future generations. It could provide a general argument for growth(or for using up resources) only if it is assumed that these sorts of investment are immutably related to growth (or resource use).

Finally, mention should be made of the following all-too-real dilemma. Consider a country which can maintain its people at subsistence only by overworking its land, thereby reducing M.S.Y. [53]. With constant resource productivity, such a policy clearly leads to disaster in the long term, especially if we add in population growth. The country faces a choice between starvation today and much worse starvation tomorrow. Technical progress and substitution may alleviate the future situation, but prospects are, as we have seen, uncertain and controversial. These possibilities transform the choice to one between certain starvation on a small scale today and the possibility (probability?) of much worse starvation tomorrow. It is an agonising choice, which most societies prefer to avoid by taking an optimistic view of the future.

OPTIMAL RESOURCE USE

Presumably most people would agree that the gloomier Doom scenarios represent a non-optimal use of resources. But what constitutes an optimal pattern of use over time? Would a policy of minimum depletion necessarily constitute an optimal pattern? We shall again pursue the questions through a series of models of increasing complexity.

[1] However, there is some evidence that, over a certain range, population growth is inversely related to consumption. If so, increasing present consumption in such countries could provide an important long-run alleviation to the resource problem. However the determinants of population growth are poorly understood, and in particular it is not clear whether consumption *per se* is an important factor, as opposed to certain correlates (e.g. education, family planning) [102]; the distinction is crucial.

46

The simplest model is the so-called cake-eating model, first studied by Hotelling [61]. A finite cake (natural resources) provides an individual (mankind) with his sole means of subsistence. Consumption implies depletion, and when the cake is exhausted, life terminates.

Presumably marginal utility declines with consumption. Hence, it is clear that, in the absence of myopia or other forms of 'pure time preference', a *constant* rate of consumption will be optimal. (For, if consumption in period A exceeds that in period B, utility may be increased by transferring consumption from A to B where the marginal utility is higher.) It is less clear what that rate should be. Longevity is maximised by a frugal policy of subsistence. At the other extreme, the whole 'cake' could be gobbled immediately – life would be short and sweet. In general there is a continuous trade-off between longevity and standard of living. The preoccupation of some economists with optimal dates for the end of the world may well be thought odd, but it is an issue which may be central to the resources question and which is posed very clearly in this simple model. A complicating factor which transforms an issue of preference into one of morality is that a high standard of living now may cut short the life not of the current generation, but of its successors. Does this strengthen or weaken the case for frugality?

There are, however, a number of modifications of the model which serve partially to remove this conflict. The simplest is to assume that life is anyway limited by other factors (e.g. cooling of the sun or the inevitability of nuclear holocaust). The cake may then be sufficiently large to maintain an above-subsistence standard of living for the allotted span – although there will still be the choice of higher consumption and a still shorter life.

The second way, as discussed by Dasgupta and Heal [59], is to introduce a second, *renewable*, resource which yields, indefinitely, a maximum consumption flow (which must be assumed to be above subsistence). When the cake is exhausted, the individual can still use this substitute resource. Recycling the 'exhaustible' resource could also be viewed in this light. The exhaustible resource is then said to be 'inessential'. It now becomes optimal to spread consumption equally over the life-span

47

(infinitely thinly if the life-span is infinite). This model suggests that, provided renewable resources are sufficient to sustain life, an exhaustible resource should be depleted very slowly. This perhaps represents rather well the mental model of some conservationists.

Dasgupta and Heal make a further and rather more questionable modification to the simple cake-eating model; future utilities are discounted, introducing pure time preference. The effect is obviously to give greater weight to earlier consumption, and not surprisingly, the optimal plan involves initially high consumption and resource use falling (exponentially) until the resource is exhausted. Conservationists will tend to comment that this is just what is happening – excessive resource depletion, stemming from a morally indefensible discounting of the future.[1]

The cake-eating model allows neither for technical progress nor capital accumulation. The former may be incorporated quite simply by allowing the ratio of consumption to resource use to increase over time. In the absence of pure time preference, consumption must now rise over time. Resource use may rise initially but eventually must fall, for were it to continue to rise until the moment of exhaustion, there would be a sudden drop in consumption, which would clearly be sub-optimal. Consumption rises despite the fall in resources use, due to the rise in resource productivity. Whether resources are ever exhausted (in finite time) depends on the exact specification of the model.

A more radical change with rather similar effects, however, is to introduce capital accumulation [59]. Production (and potential consumption) then depends both on resources R, and the capital stock K. This has a twofold significance: first, present activity affects the future in two ways – by depleting R (adverse) and by increasing K (favourable). Secondly, capital provides at least a partial substitute for resources. Indeed, Dasgupta and

[1] All the conventional reasons for discounting the future are absent here. Diminishing marginal utility is specifically allowed for – it is utilities, not merely consumptions, that are being discounted; and there is no uncertainty. Discounting, in this model, represents pure time preference.

Heal consider the possibility that output can be produced from capital alone without any (direct) resource inputs. Capital then amounts to a man-made renewable resource and R becomes inessential. In this case, it can be shown that it will be optimal to deplete resources fully in finite time. If, on the other hand, some direct resource input remains essential to production, then indefinite stretching of the resource becomes optimal.

Dasgupta and Heal have further elaborated the model to embrace technical progress, capital accumulation and uncertainty. Such extensions lead to great complexity and their value must be subject to rapidly diminishing returns. For it is clear, from the factors already considered, that even the general shape of the optimal path depends crucially on the details of the model. Some general properties of the optimum path may be quoted:

(i) *Consumption* will follow a monotonic trend but whether this is upward or downward depends on the balance of the following considerations: technical progress and possibilities for capital substitution (upward forces); and present-biased time preference and most forms of uncertainty (downward forces).

(ii) *Resource use* must eventually decline (that much is obvious from the finiteness of the total stock) but may (optimally) rise first. It may be optimal to deplete exhaustible resources fully in a finite time (if technical progress and substitution possibilities are sufficiently strong).

(iii) *Resource rents* will rise at a rate equal to the interest rate [60].

THE INCENTIVES TO CONSERVATION

Optimists place great reliance in the price mechanism as providing an incentive to conservation [e.g. 30, 50, 56]. Whenever a (marketed) resource product becomes scarce, its price will tend to rise. This will provide incentives to economise on its use, to seek substitute products and processes, to prospect for new supplies and to recycle old ones; anticipated scarcities will induce resource owners to reduce the rate of extraction in expectation of future price increases. Optimists stress these mechanisms as a vehicle for continued growth, but they should also provide a smooth transition from rapid growth to the steady state, should resource scarcity make this necessary (cf. [58]).

Of course, perfect markets combined with perfect 'rationality' will produce the optimum amount of conservation; and it must be possible to explain excessive depletion in terms of specific sources of market failure or failures in rationality. Consider first resources in private ownership whose products are marketed (most minerals and fuels fall within this category) [60, 62].

First, there is the argument that due to myopia, risk aversion, monopoly in capital markets and neglect of future generations, the market gives excessive weight to present costs and benefits. This argument was used by Tobin to justify a more rapid rate of investment in man-made capital (see p. 27) and is used by resource pessimists to justify a slower rate of disinvestment in resource capital. Indeed, as Kay and Mirrlees [62] point out, the two arguments hang together and are summed up in an assertion that the discount rate is too high.

It is perhaps not generally appreciated just how little weight is currently given to the future in investment decisions. A 10 per cent discount rate implies that the weight given to current benefits is twice that accorded to benefits seven years hence, and some 16,000 times that accorded to those accruing to our great grandchildren 100 years hence.

If the growth process is viewed solely in terms of technical progress and the accumulation of man-made capital (as in Tobin's model) such heavy weighting could be justified in terms of the rise in living standards (twenty-fold over 100 years at 3 per cent per annum growth). But resource depletion changes this picture, at least on a pessimistic view. Rapid growth uses up resources and in the longer term causes living standards to fall. Heavy discounting of the future is no longer justified.

The suggestion that a lowering of the discount rate is required to encourage resource conservation may seem paradoxical. For we have become accustomed to the idea that a low discount rate promotes growth, which surely aggravates the resource problem. However, this idea is derived from a capital theory which takes no account of resource depletion. In fact a lowering of the discount rate will both encourage investment in man-made capital and discourage resource depletion. There will thus be two opposing effects on growth in G.N.P. But, more important, the structure of output will be changed, away from, for example, consumption and resource-intensive products and processes, and towards, for example, resource-saving investment and recycling.

A second group of arguments stems from the great uncertainty surrounding future projects. Current decisions by resource holders and others must be based on *expected* future prices which are unknown and indeed depend partly on the decisions in question. Technically, this gives rise to the problem of secondary uncertainty [60]. In practice, decision-makers are likely to form their expectations in a rather naive manner by projecting current trends. Optimally, the prices of resource products will often follow a falling trend at first, due to falling exploitation costs, followed by a rising one as the effect of scarcity predominates. It is argued [60, 63] that resource-owners are likely not to anticipate this turning point. They will continue to deplete resource excessively and by this action will indeed for a time depress the price, thereby validating their expectations. For a time, until decision-makers finally appreciate the true situation, prices will be too low and rates of extraction too fast. However, Kay and Mirrlees [62] show that, until the last few decades of the life of a resource, expected *prices* play a surprisingly small part in determining extraction rates, extraction *costs* being the dominant consideration. The reason for this finding turns out to be the small weight accorded to the future using conventional rates of discount. We have just suggested, however, that these rates are (on a pessimistic view) too high.

There is also the risk of Doom. Pessimism increases the rate o exploitation, which consequently increases the risk of Doom. In this case, the private attitude to risk is clearly socially suboptimal.

It must be emphasised that our assessment of these arguments must be closely bound up with our assessment of resource adequacy. For, on an optimistic view, the discount rate is not necessarily too high and in this case, faulty estimation of future prices is not a serious source of bias. However, acceptance of Meade's view of Doomrisk (p. 45) requires us to place a high weight on the implications of the pessimistic view.

Finally, mention should be made of one reason – monopoly pricing – why resource exploitation may be too low. Kay and Mirrlees [62] suggest that this may sometimes be the dominant factor, particularly in the currently topical case of oil.

COMMON RESOURCES, EXTERNALITIES AND E-GOODS

So far, attention has been focused exclusively on privately owned resources, viewed solely as inputs to the productive process. Externality problems are definitionally absent.

Some resources are however owned 'in common' or, in plainer English, not owned by anyone. It is easily seen that such resources are liable to excessive depletion. Commercial fishing provides a classic example [57]; typically, neither the water nor the fish are owned, and accordingly each fisherman will regard the depletion of the stock only in so far as it affects his own activities. If there are n fishermen, the individual will bear but $1/n$th of the total costs of depletion; the rest are external costs which he will ignore. Of course, it may be that, even if all fishermen operate on these principles, the total catch still falls short of M.S.Y. If so there is no depletion and no external costs; fish are a free good. With demographic and economic growth, it is to be expected that (in the absence of effective regulation) common resource problems will become increasingly serious.

Non-renewable resources owned in common will always be overexploited. An important example is the gas- or oil-field permeated by a number of rival boreholes (as occurs in the North Sea, America and elsewhere). The situation is aggravated by the adverse dependence of the amount of oil recoverable and the rate of extraction.

Some resources have more than one productive use. For example, a lake may be used both for fishing and as a dumping ground for industrial wastes. In this example, the quality of the lake as a fishery is adversely affected by dumping (above a certain level) but not vice versa.

Many resources yield E-goods. It will be convenient to term such resources E-resources, and resources that yield M-goods

52

M-resources.[1] Many resources yield both and are thus simultaneously E-resources and M-resources. This is a source of serious conflict.

E-resources are necessarily liable to common resource problems because, definitionally, the E-goods which they provide are not marketed. Recreational fishing provides an example closely paralleling the commercial fishing example considered above. Another problem which is causing increasing concern is the destruction of beauty spots by excessive trampling. In such cases, the resource provides an M.S.Y., just like an M-resource. If demand (at the zero price) exceeds this, a common resource problem arises.

Now consider resources which yield both M-goods and E-goods. Sometimes the resource may be unowned, as when commercial and recreational fishermen – and perhaps industrial and domestic polluters also – operate in the same lake. No new issues arise. In other cases, a privately owned resource yields M-goods to the owner and E-goods to the public at large. In the absence of regulations, or conceivably altruism, the resource will be managed without regard to the latter. Sometimes, there will be a measure of complementarity between the M-goods and the E-goods produced; a forest, for example, provides both timber and beauty and the provision of one will provide the other as a by-product; even in this case, however, the type of wood planted and the felling regimes adopted are likely to be those that do not entirely maximise the visual quality of the forest. The uses may be far more incompatible, as when a waterfall is put in a pipe and used to generate electricity; in this case, the resource is renewable in both capacities. Often, however, it is non-renewable in its productive capacity as when a hillside provides a renewable landscape or non-renewable stone. Extraction of the stone depletes both the stock of stone and the quality of the landscape.

Some common resource/externality effects are exceedingly complicated because of the diversity of their effects. Consider

[1] Several models [35, 36, 38] employ this distinction between productive and environmental resources. Vousden [67] introduces a 'conservation motive' into an otherwise orthodox resource model, implying that resources yield also environmental services.

pesticide spraying which leads to the emergence of more virulent pests and a destruction of predators. This has a direct effect on farmers and as such constitutes a straightforward common resource problem – the resource 'crop resistance' is overworked and thereby depleted. But it also has much more far-reaching effects throughout the eco-system. For example, fish yields and human health are put at risk and processes of photosynthesis may be interfered with [41, 42]. Possible climatic effects of heat output, air pollution and supersonic flight and reductions in species diversity[1] (brought about by monoculture, land clearance, pesticides, etc.) provide further examples of common resource problems which are very broad and possibly very important [39, 41, 48].

[1] Apart from biological and general interest, there is an ecological argument that diversity is a source of stability; a reduction in this diversity, it is suggested, increases the risk of a breakdown in the complex life-support systems, which would spell global catastrophe [58, 46, 104].

5 Policies for Environmental Protection

Approaches to environmental problems vary widely. It is neither possible in a short chapter nor indeed relevant to our main theme to present a rounded survey. Rather, we shall attempt to highlight certain issues which are especially related to the growth–environment controversy. We shall contrast two paradigm positions, which we may label 'orthodox' and 'radical'. According to the orthodox school, environmental problems are readily handled by standard economic theory demanding at most a shift of emphasis; more specifically such problems are viewed as due primarily to externalities and accordingly a favoured remedy is to 'internalise' the costs of environmental damage by making the perpetrator bear the social costs of pollution himself. According to the radical school, the niceties of the orthodox analysis are misleading and the measures indicated insufficient to prevent a disastrous deterioration of the environment; some of this school advance Draconian across-the-board measures such as a total halt to economic growth.

THE ORTHODOX ANALYSIS

We begin then by outlining the orthodox analysis of externalities. Consider a typical environmental problem, a factory discharging effluents into a river. To present the analysis in its most appealing form, attention is confined initially to the additional purification costs imposed on downstream factories and water authorities. These are shown as *damage costs* in Fig. 10 (p. 56). However there are also costs involved in reducing or eliminating the discharges, for this will involve cutting back output, adopting cleaner, and in general more expensive, technology or installing additional plant to purify the effluent. These additional costs

55

are shown as *control costs* in Fig. 10. In Fig. 10(*a*) *total* damage and control costs are plotted, while in Fig. 10(*b*), the same information is shown on a *marginal* basis. The reader should satisfy himself as to the general shape of these functions, which is indeed crucial to the orthodox analysis which follows.

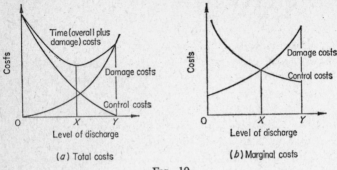

FIG. 10

Whereas the control costs fall on the polluter, the damage costs fall on others; the latter are 'external' to the offending firm, which will thus have no incentive to take them into account in planning its scale and techniques of production. The firm may be expected to minimise its *control* costs, which is seen from Fig. 10(*a*) to involve a discharge of 0Y.

The social problem is to reduce discharges not to zero but to the optimum level 0X where the *sum* of the control costs and the damage costs is minimised. To the left of X, the benefits of any further reduction in pollution damage is outweighed by the additional costs of pollution control. At the optimum point X, *marginal* control costs equal *marginal* damage costs, as shown in Fig. 10(*b*).

Conceptually, the simplest way of reaching the social optimum is to legislate a maximum pollution level equal to 0X. Under this constraint, the firm will act in a socially optimum way.[1] However, this method is rather exacting in its informational requirements, in that it requires the authorities to ascertain not

[1] This discussion of course assumes that river pollution is the only source of market failure, and ignores also 'irrationality' and income distribution problems (see pp. 67–76).

only the damage function (any policy requires *some* view to be taken about pollution damage) but also the control function.

An alternative method, which does not demand this information is the 'fiscal' method, which involves levying a tax equal to the marginal social cost of pollution.[1] This 'internalises' the external pollution cost, bringing private and social costs into equality, so that the private optimum and social optimum now coincide. To operate such a policy, the authorities need information about the social damage only, leaving the factory itself to take into account the private control costs. The method thus follows the free market principle of maximum decentralisation of decision-making.

However the determination and implementation of an appropriate tax policy are neither simple nor costless. First, the marginal damage and hence the appropriate level of the tax will in general depend on the level of emission of the firm in question. If then the tax is set to correspond to the current emission level, the firm will respond by cutting back its effluent and at the new level the tax will be too high. The problem is further compounded if the tax is to apply to a number of factories on the same stream, since the marginal damage due to effluents from any one source is highly dependent on stream quality and hence on effluents from other sources. There will in general be a set of taxes which generates levels of emission at which marginal rates of damage equal the taxes, and the authorities may attempt to find these by a process of trial and error. But the 'errors' meanwhile may be rather large and troublesome [6, 69].

Secondly, severe problems arise in estimating the damage function. So far attention has been confined to effects which are readily measurable in monetary terms. But water pollution may also result in loss of amenity to bathers, anglers and walkers along the river bank. In principle such losses may be valued in terms of the minimum payment necessary to induce those concerned willingly to accept them; in practice, valuation is frequently so difficult that the losses in question are brushed aside as 'intangibles'. Water pollution may also set in train a complex

[1] Various other methods have been proposed, for example the issue of marketable licences to pollute and the subsidisation of anti-pollution equipment (see [71] or [78] for a general review).

sequence of ecological effects, very difficult to predict or evaluate but not necessarily unimportant. Some writers [69] indeed reject any attempt at estimating the damage function; they propose instead setting standards of stream quality arbitrarily and using prices to allocate the corresponding *overall* level of discharges among different sources.

Thirdly, there is the so-called 'Deadweight Loss', that is the costs of estimating pollution damage, of measuring emissions, collecting the taxes and countering evasion, as well as certain burdens on the factories. (The optimal regulatory scheme involves, as we saw, even greater Deadweight Loss.) The costs of attaining the otherwise optimal point X are not represented in the diagram. It is no accident that one of the commonest ways of combating environmental problems is the simple one of outright prohibition. This involves an apparently excessive reduction in external costs, but this may be preferable not only to zero reduction, but also, when Deadweight Loss is taken into account, to the 'ideal' reduction to $0X$.

Environmental problems are typically far more complex than the above discussion indicates. Stream quality, for example, is a function of not one pollutant but many, and each individual pollutant would ideally have to be the subject of a specific regulation or tax. Moreover the effects of individual pollutants interact: the presence of one can aggravate the effect of another, or it can neutralise it (see e.g. [42]). Again the precise location of a factory, temperature and stream level will be among other determinants of the effects of a particular discharge. An 'ideal' structure of taxes or regulations would distinguish between these various conditions. An 'ideal' structure would multiply prodigiously all the complications discussed above. In other words, while optimum pollution levels entail a complex tax (or regulation) structure, when Deadweight Loss is taken into account the optimum tax structure is a relatively simple one, entailing substantial deviation from the theoretical optimum.

River pollution is a public bad, which could be alleviated by the provision of a public good in the form of public purification facilities. Such provision might achieve substantial economies of scale and is not subject to the costs and difficulties of enforcement. Domestic sewage is a striking example. On the

58

other hand, modifying production techniques or producing different goods or the same goods in different places may be preferable to either public or at-source purification. The two approaches are not mutually exclusive; public purification facilities could be combined with pollution taxes – the latter would then reflect the additional purification costs plus any changes in residual pollution.

There would be no financial returns from a purification plant, because of its public good characteristics[1] (see Chapter 2). The installation of such a plant would have to be assessed by some technique such as cost–benefit analysis. This would involve estimating and evaluating all the benefits of improved stream quality – to anglers, bathers, factories, etc. These problems are precisely those already encountered in deriving optimal pollution taxes.

SOME CRITICISMS

The orthodox view attributes environmental deterioration[2] largely to a failure to pursue the above ideas (not in themselves expecially novel, e.g. [107]) with sufficient vigour. Despite the many difficulties discussed, they consider that crude policies could be devised *ad hoc* to prevent undue further deterioration. They see them as obviating the need for more extreme policies such as reducing or halting economic growth. To some extent, however, it is misleading to regard environmental policies of this sort as *alternatives* to reducing growth since this would be their incidental effect. Benefits which are not included in G.N.P. would be traded for other (smaller) benefits which are. G.N.P. would fall and, during the period of transition to such policies, growth would fall, probably substantially (see p. 23). Therefore the path of G.N.P. would remain well below that in the absence

[1] The plant could be 'financed' from levies on the polluters, as on the Ruhr [73], or alternatively on the beneficiaries from the plant. These levies would, however, need to be compulsory and hence would not reflect 'willingness to pay'. There are no grounds for supposing such means of financing to be 'efficient'.

[2] Some maintain that there has been no deterioration [15] or that such deterioration which has occurred is outweighed by the concomitant material gains [21, 30].

of such policies, although the ultimate effect on the growth rate is not clear. But the case for arguing the superiority of such measures over *macro-economic* approaches seems strong. Nevertheless it has been strenuously opposed [46, 72, 76].

To some extent, this controversy turns upon a terminological confusion. Formally, the above analyses are simply implications of a policy of pursuing maximum benefit. These critics can hardly object to that! Though this is not always made sufficiently clear, their criticisms relate to the kinds of criteria invariably used in deriving net benefits. Their objections are both positive and normative.

First, these are partial equilibrium techniques operated within a general context of *ceteris paribus*. On apparently sound practical grounds, remoter costs and benefits are invariably ignored. This would not matter if the omitted items tended to cancel out, but since most environmental effects are adverse and, moreover, interacting, this is unlikely to be the case. In addition many items (e.g. scenic beauty) are omitted because of difficulties of monetary evaluation.

Secondly, in the interests of 'objectivity', orthodox analysis customarily employs a 'willingness-to-pay' criterion of evaluation, possibly adjusted for income distribution. This will be inappropriate in the face of ignorance or irrationality. Many environmental effects may not be widely appreciated and willingness to pay will be correspondingly low.

In many such cases, the environmental effects are controversial. Some writers consider that, provided appropriate action is taken to combat the more obvious and direct kinds of externality, even cumulative degradation of the environment should not pose problems beyond the capacity of advancing technology to solve [47]. The critics just cited are less optimistic, however, and argue that any pollution contributes a shock to the system, a potential source of ecological instability and a risk not only to human well-being but to the very survival of the species [42, 76].

In the face of disagreements among experts, the attitude taken to risk, and especially survival risk, is crucial. The willingness-to-pay criterion automatically adopts the attitude (to *perceived* risk of course) of the current generation. Pearce, on the other hand, considers that minimising survival risk should be the paramount consideration and that environmental shocks should be avoided at all costs [76]. This is an extreme view, involving zero pollution and, if followed immediately, a sharp cut back in material consumption.[1] One might argue that it was worth trading some material consumption for a small (but how small?) risk of species demise.

Finally there is the related issue of the interests of future generations, who will bear much of the burden of cumulative pollution and of the risks just discussed. Formally, by employing a high discount rate and relatively short horizons, standard cost–benefit analysis gives little weight to such interests. But if environmental burdens and risks are important, their interests would not be served simply by lowering the discount rate and extending horizons. The omission of the burdens and risks is also crucial.

THE ZERO-GROWTH SCHOOL

Some writers see a complete halt to economic (and demographic) growth as the only satisfactory answer to the environmental problem.[2] Since 'zero growth' is an essentially macro-economic concept, let us first examine the question in a macro-economic context.

First, it should be pointed out that 'zero' is a rather special rate of growth, requiring a special justification. For example our macro-economic discussion suggested that it might be beneficial to reduce the growth in material goods production, but there

[1] A more acceptable strategy might be to hold consumption constant and use the fruits of technical advance to reduce pollution, eventually to zero. To accept such a strategy would be to admit the validity of the trade-off argument given in the text. In poor countries, an immediate cessation of pesticide pollution may well increase deaths from starvation in the short run.

[2] Zero growth here is interpreted literally, in terms of $G.N.P.$ Some authors [2, 40, 43, 76] emphasise that *resource depletion* and *persistent pollution* must eventually fall to zero in the stationary state economy. This leaves open whether the corresponding level of production is higher or lower than the current one. Also the environmental constraints do not necessarily imply a constant level of $G.N.P.$, especially in the presence of technical progress.

61

was little to warrant the idea that zero growth might be optimal.

The general idea is of course that resources place a limit on sustainable production (Chapter 4). Hence the rise in G.N.P. must sooner or later flatten off. Furthermore, since no-one has much idea of the exact position of the limit, it might be wise to halt growth immediately. There are however grounds *both* for thinking that such a policy might be unnecessarily severe *and* that it might be inadequate. On the one hand technical advance might progressively push back the limit (Chapter 4), and on the other, the world may already be exceeding sustainable production limits. Deteriorating soil fertility, persistent pollution, and inevitably, depletion of 'non-renewable' resources result even from present production levels.

However the case for zero growth becomes stronger if there is a heavy disutility attached to a *fall* in aggregate consumption. This is a fairly plausible hypothesis, with some empirical support (e.g. [83]), and one that is frequently adopted in macro-economic optimising models (the constraint $C_t - C_{t-1} \geqslant 0$ is applied). Negative growth rates thus involve heavy disutility now, while positive growth rates increase the risk that consumption will subsequently have to be cut back.

An alternative justification for zero growth is that there is a heavy disutility associated with *change* or in striving for change. If this disutility is weak, it provides a source of asymmetry between consumption rises and falls, similar to that discussed in the previous paragraph. If strong, it may offset the benefits of growth altogether, even if there is no risk of a subsequent fall. Inevitably growth involves *changes* in the physical and cultural environment not merely an expansion in material consumption. Even if a dispassionate observer regards the new environment as superior to the old, the dynamic process of change can be an uncomfortable one for large sectors of the population, especially the old [28, 43, 112].

A major theme of the environmentalists' attack on growth, and of this book, is the inadequacy of the G.N.P. statistic as a welfare measure. But it is equally inadequate, and for much the same reasons, as an indicator of environmental degradation. It is an aggregate of numerous widely disparate goods and services with widely disparate impacts on the environment. Some acti-

62

vities (car production and use) are highly pollutive, others (symphony concerts) hardly at all; yet others (tree planting) hopefully improve the environment. A policy conceived in terms of such an aggregate, whether it be for a maximal growth rate or a zero one, is too simple [24, 30, 32].

It is, of course, precisely because of the enormous complexity of environmental problems that over-simple approaches are adopted. We see that orthodox partial equilibrium approaches fail in so far as they fail to take due account of systems effects, and that macro-economics fail in that they ignore heterogeneity. It is easy to assert that what is needed is a complete but dis-aggregated model of the world so that effects of individual activities can be fully explored. No model approaching the required complexity could conceivably be constructed, how-ever, and inevitably we act in considerable ignorance.

Let us draw some conclusions from the above discussion:

(1) There are numerous individual, though interrelated, aspects of the environmental problem, so that numerous indi-vidual environmental policies are required.

(2) Unless a very extreme strategy is adopted (e.g. no change at all) each case must inevitably be decided on its merits.

(3) Recognition must be given to the interdependence be-tween environmental effects. Broad systems models may be helpful in doing this (the materials balance approach, developed by Ayres and Kneese [68] should be mentioned), but cannot be sufficiently detailed to provide more than general guidelines for any specific policy.

(4) There is a serious danger that evaluations of costs and benefits on which micro-evaluations are inevitably based will be biased towards excessive environmental damage due to: (a) omission of 'intangibles'; (b) omission of many individually small but re-enforcing items; (c) disutilities associated with change; and (d) asymmetries in the pay-off function.[1]

(5) Careful attention must be paid to the value judgements inevitably implicit in evaluation. 'Willingness to pay' does *not* provide an objective value-free criterion.

[1] It is usual to work with 'most likely' i.e. modal outcomes. An improvement is to use mean or expected outcomes. However this is not appropriate if society is risk-averse.

63

6 Distribution

Distributional considerations have so far been ignored – swept under the carpet by the useful expository device of the community indifference curve. This allowed us to concentrate on the allocational aspects of the growth–environment controversy.

However both growth and environmental policies can have important distributional implications and distributional questions have loomed large in the controversies. This chapter is divided into four sections. In the first we concentrate on how far growth promotes a more equitable distribution of M-goods. In the second we consider the distribution of environmental quality and how this is affected by alternative measures for environmental protection. The third is concerned with certain controversies over the imposition of environmental standards in Third World countries, the fourth is concerned with intergenerational equity.

GROWTH AND THE DISTRIBUTION OF M-GOODS

Growth-men argue that growth is the major instrument for raising the living standards of the poor. With neutral technical progress, capital accumulation will tend to raise both the real wage and the share of wage incomes in G.N.P. The position of the poor is improved both absolutely and relatively. However with labour-saving technical progress (a probable result of the rise in the real wage), this conclusion breaks down. There have been long periods of acute misery brought about by mechanisation forcing down the real wage – and also leading to unemployment. Even neutral technical progress can lead to serious structural unemployment while the economy adjusts painfully to the change.

However the growth-men's argument does not rest solely on market processes. Government policy is of course a major determinant of distribution, and governments can ensure that a high proportion of the proceeds of growth are directed toward the poor. In a stationary economy, the incomes of the poor can be increased only by reducing those of the rich. This is painful for the rich, accustomed as they are to affluent living styles, and consequently politically difficult; in a growing economy, incomes of the poor can be increased both absolutely and relatively, without any drop in the incomes of the rich [21, 26].

Historically, it is argued, incomes of most sections of most countries have, at least over long periods, risen with national income. The major current exception concerns Third World countries where, despite growth in national income per head, large sections of the population continue to eke out a subsistence living and death from malnutrition remains common. Indeed in several Third World countries the numbers and even the proportions living at subsistence may be rising. This may be explicable not only in terms of inadequate distributional policies but also in terms of differential fertility rates. The conventional wisdom is nevertheless that the problem of malnutrition can be cured only by still faster growth, at a rate fast enough to offset the adverse factors just mentioned.

Whether the incomes of the poor have increased *relatively* is more controversial.[1] In general, income is undeniably more equally distributed than say in the Middle Ages in advanced countries, but it is difficult to distinguish growth (as opposed to, say, democratisation[2]) as the fundamental factor. Several writers have suggested that, both in Britain and the U.S., postwar growth has had virtually no impact on certain disadvantaged groups, thus leading to a deterioration in their relative position.

There is considerable disagreement over trends in the intercountry distribution of income; most writers (e.g. [79]) speak

[1] In so far as marginal utility declines with income, an improvement in income distribution understates the improvement in utility distribution. Indeed it would be possible, as G.N.P. rises, for income to become more unequal and at the same time utility to become more equal.

[2] Characteristically, Beckerman [15] uses the expression '*growth in democratic institutions*' to give a subliminal boost to his pro-growth position!

of a widening gap, but a recent study [80] indicates that there may have been a (very small) improvement.

Certainly, whatever the effects on the poor, the living standards of the richer countries and richer sections (though perhaps not the very richest) of individual countries have risen absolutely. This, of itself, increases inequality. In particular if, because of resource limitations, growth must eventually stop, then allowing the incomes of the rich to increase becomes a positive barrier to equality. For, as the growth-men themselves argue, it is always more painful and more difficult to reduce someone's income from a given level than to prevent it from ever reaching that level. Thus if 'limits to growth' are accepted, then to avoid the difficulties of levelling down later, it becomes vitally important to level up now. This means reducing, and even eliminating, growth in the incomes of the rich [33].

An important consideration is clearly how far individual welfare depends on *absolute* and how far on *relative* income: the importance of the relative income effect (which does not depend solely on 'envy') has been discussed by Duesenberry [83] and Mishan [28] and is receiving increasing acceptance. While its implications are generally ignored, its importance has rarely been challenged. A related phenomenon is that the growth process may lead to an expansion of wants and a dissatisfaction with current standards [98, 28].

It will be observed that, in common with so many pro-growth arguments, growth has been taken as exogenous (as in Chapter 2). The argument may be widened to bring in the effects on distribution of intertemporal choice. First, whatever the benefits on distribution of higher consumption in the future (as above) they are offset by the effects of lower consumption in the current period. Second, cross-sectionwise the marginal propensity to save increases with income. Hence growth and income redistribution are in direct conflict. More fundamentally, the optimum rate of growth depends on distribution; for the poor will place relatively more weight on present consumption (as evidenced by their lower marginal propensity to save). The more weight is given to the preferences of the poor, the more appropriate will a slow rate of growth become.

THE DISTRIBUTION OF E-GOODS

E-goods are, definitionally, public goods. This does not imply, however, that all benefit equally from a high quality environment. In the first place valuations of environmental quality relative to material goods varies widely from person to person. This is partly a matter of taste (for example, sensitivity to noise is known to vary widely), partly a matter of welfare levels. There is an argument, which we shall shortly consider, that poor people place a relatively low importance on environmental quality.

Secondly, environmental quality is not a homogeneous commodity. Not only are there many aspects of environmental quality (noise, sulphur pollution, carbon monoxide pollution, etc.) but more significantly each varies widely from locality to locality, and the environmental effects of an activity will generally be particularly concentrated in a small number of nearby localities.[1] Since tastes vary, this variation in attributes of environmental quality does, to some extent, allow individuals an opportunity to choose an environment to suit their particular preferences. Such choice is however severely limited by immobility in the face of environmental changes.

Despite variations in tastes, there are some environments which most would accept as preferable to some others. For example, most would prefer their houses to adjoin a spacious park than a smoky industrial estate. As a result of this general preference, the former houses command a higher price which the affluent find easier to afford.

If incomes were equal but the marginal rate of substitution between E-goods and M-goods varied widely, then consumption of E-goods and M-goods would be negatively correlated. If, on the other hand, tastes were uniform but incomes unequal, then consumption of E-goods and M-goods would be positively

[1] However, if the pollutant is persistent (e.g. D.D.T., heavy metals), it is likely to progress rapidly through the eco-system, giving rise to problems of more than local significance. If pessimists are to be believed, such problems are of dominating importance, possibly leading to the extinction of life on the planet [44].

67

correlated.[1] Despite substantial taste variations, casual observation suggests that the income effect is generally dominant.

That environmental quality is inequitably distributed is perhaps scarcely in dispute. The issue is rather how far measures for environmental protection and improvement affect distribution. Mishan [28, 29] insists that the environmental case can be developed in terms of externalities (as in the previous chapters of this book) and is quite independent of distributional considerations. Formally this position is unassailable. Not only are the arguments valid when income is equally distributed but it will always be optimal to pursue allocationally correct policies, compensating for undesirable distribution effects by lump-sum transfers, assuming these to be available and costless. In practice, of course, lump-sum transfers are generally not feasible, and resort must be had to non-lump-sum methods of redistribution, such as income tax. These involve departures from optimality which could, in principle, be as serious as the original distortions which the environmental policies are designed to correct. Indeed one might insist that environmental policies should be considered along with other sub-optimal instruments as a method of achieving a more equitable distribution of welfare.

However the view that environmental quality is predominantly the concern of the rich [15, 16, 18, 82] also appears to be an unhelpful and misleading generalisation. In the simplest case of a universal environmental good and uniform tastes there is no clear connection between distribution and the allocationally optimum of environmental quality. Expenditure to improve the environment, will of itself tend to be more of benefit to the rich (they would be prepared to pay more for the improvement) but the *overall* impact depends also on how the expenditure is financed; there is a strong expectation that the rich will bear a major share of the cost.

However in this context, the heterogeneity of environmental goods is important. They range from matters of aesthetics (e.g. scenic beauty) to matters of life and death (e.g. more serious forms of pollution). The rich will tend to avoid localities subject

---

[1] A complicating factor may be a systematic relationship between preference maps and incomes (endogenous wants again).

to the latter problem, which will be peopled entirely by the poor. Rich environmentalists will, unless altruistic, concentrate on the environmental problems (scenic beauty) affecting their own locality. The necessarily poor inhabitants of localities suffering from the latter problem will care relatively little for scenic beauty but, if sufficiently well informed, will care much about pollution. Since the rich tend to be more vocal and influential, the former problems may receive undue prominence, while the latter are neglected.

Little more can usefully be said in general. In practice much will depend on the instruments used for environmental protection. Accordingly we turn now to a consideration of the distributional impact of specific types of environmental policy.

The curtailment of adverse externalities. Three methods have been suggested: (i) taxation; (ii) physical controls; and (iii) subsidies for reduction of the offence (e.g. installation of non-pollutive equipment).

There are three distributional effects to be considered. The first stems from the curtailment of the activity *per se*. This represents a gain to the sufferer, and a loss to the perpetrator. Sometimes, the same people may be both sufferers and perpetrators. For example, motorists both cause, and then suffer, congestion; they would suffer from any curtailment of their activities but would gain from the associated reduction in congestion. Whether on balance they gain or lose depends on a number of factors including the initial level of congestion [113]. In any event, these gains and losses are, definitionally, independent of the means by which the externality is controlled.

The second and most controversial effect concerns the differential impact on different perpetrators. It is often argued (e.g. [110]) that restriction by taxation has least impact on the rich who can most easily afford to pay the tax, and is hence undesirable on distributional grounds. Consider this argument, with specific reference to motoring, to which it is most commonly applied. Now, the income elasticity of motoring is greater than one (motoring is thus a 'luxury'). Hence, initially, the rich motorist will bear the largest tax burden, not only absolutely, but proportionately to income. Such a tax, in common with

69

other luxury taxes, would normally be deemed progressive. All motorists, both rich and poor, will tend to avoid the tax by cutting back on motoring (as intended in this case); but in general there seems no reason to expect the poorer motorist to make greater proportional cuts than his richer colleague, except that the marginal motorist may find it no longer economic to keep a car at all.

These effects may be compared with those of controls. It is at once apparent that much will depend on the kind of control adopted. Two paradigm cases will be considered, one where the offending activities are cut *pro rata*, the second where a permitted level of activity is specified which is to apply uniformly to all. With the first form of control, richer people will tend to be permitted higher activity levels, although they will also suffer the largest (absolute) cut-backs. The pattern of consumption is indeed likely to be broadly similar to that under control by taxation. The main difference is that control by taxation involves a larger tax burden for the rich and in this respect is more equitable.

Specification of uniform activity levels on the other hand will tend to benefit the poor more than either of the other methods, except that under control by taxation the rich will suffer a tax burden absent under either method of physical control. Specification of uniform activity levels will also impinge with especial severity of those with especially strong preferences for the offending activity.

The third and final distributional effect to be considered is the budgetary impact of the measure. It is surprising how often this effect is neglected. Taxation involves an increase in government revenue allowing either a reduction in other taxes or an increase in government expenditure. The redistributive effect will clearly depend on the precise nature of the compensating budgetary changes (which range from a reduction in surtax to an increase in supplementary benefits), but there must be a general presumption that increased taxation of an affluent group (such as motorists) will be progressive. On the other hand, taxation of, say, environmental ill-effects of food production would be likely to have an adverse distributional effect (although these could easily be offset by general food subsidies). Control by physical methods will not bring in revenue and will be free from this kind of distributional effect. Control by subsidy will involve expenditure and a redistribution from the public at large to the perpetrators.

Another argument with important distributional implications is that strong environmental curbs would generate unemployment. For example pollution controls could involve insolvency and closure for some firms. Four comments are however in order:

(i) Any *general* increase in unemployment may readily be eliminated by orthodox Keynesian policies.

(ii) Structural unemployment represents a more intractable problem. Various partial remedies exist, however, such as redundancy payments, retraining schemes, regional policies or special grants to affected firms. It is also important to realise that structural unemployment is essentially a problem of adjustment to over-rapid change. Hence, at most, it constitutes an argument for gradualism in the introduction of environmental (or any other) policies.

(iii) In any case, environmental policies do not necessarily generate unemployment. For example, ecologically sound farming methods are more labour-intensive and would help to reduce rural unemployment.

(iv) The technical progress involved in the growth process is a major creator of unemployment. New fuel technologies have led to unemployment in the mines, new transport technologies to unemployment in shipyards and railway workshops. On a smaller scale, new capital-intensive machinery has frequently led to redundancy.

In short, environmental policies do not seem to constitute any special danger of unemployment.

Cost–benefit analysis. This technique allows account to be taken of market imperfections in government decision-making. Pollution, congestion, noise and other forms of environmental nuisance can be valued and thus included in calculating the *social* profitability of the project in question. It is standard practice to value environmental effects according to an estimate of willingness to pay in a hypothetical market. Thus cost–benefit

71

(like control by taxation) involves a direct attempt to combat market failure. It applies the normal criterion of the market and is aimed at achieving allocative efficiency.

The extension of the willingness-to-pay criterion beyond its normal sphere of influence may involve an extension of the inequalities which this criterion implies. This is most obviously the case where there is a choice of location for an environmentally damaging project such as a road or an airport. The affluent will naturally be willing to pay more not to have the development in question on the doorstep, so that a standard cost–benefit analysis will tend to indicate choice of a poor locality for the development.[1]

While cost–benefit attempts to follow market criteria, there is one important difference. Whereas market allocation requires actual payments to be made, with cost–benefit the payments are generally hypothetical. For example, if a motorway is routed through A rather than B – and this perhaps partly because the residents of A are poorer – residents of A become impoverished relative to those of B and are hence less willing (able) to pay when the site for an airport is considered.[2]

The distributional impact of cost–benefit should not however be exaggerated, because for informal decision criteria will also tend to favour development in poor areas. This is partly because financial costs, for example of buying land, will be lower, and partly because the poor are likely to offer less resistance. Also localities where poor people live will tend to be of poor quality (poor people live in the area because house prices are low, not the reverse); indeed, even if the area has qualities which the poor value highly, these may be given little weight by middle-

[1] Notice, for example, that time savings are generally valued in relation to earnings and noise in relation to property values. The textual point is valid whether disbenefits are measured by 'willingness to pay not to have the development' or 'minimum compensation required for the project to be acceptable'.

[2] I am indebted to my colleague, Martin Slater, for this point. Notice also an inconsistency in cost–benefit analysis, in that the locational decisions concerning the siting of the airport and motorway will in general depend whether they are considered together or sequentially.

class planners. All in all, decision-makers will tend to feel that less of value is destroyed if the poor area is chosen for the development. Cost–benefit analysis will do little more than formalise these tendencies, which indeed have some merit despite their unfortunate distributional implications [24].

Arguably, cost–benefit does little more than give formal expression to some of these tendencies, at the same time providing means of correction, reviewed by Pearce in [105]. One method is to incorporate distributional judgements into the valuation procedure by weighting cost–benefits according to the income (or welfare level) of the sufferer/beneficiary. Not only the environmental effects but also the ordinary financial effects may be adjusted in this way. It should be emphasised that the stronger the differential weighting, the greater will be the departure from allocative efficiency. Consideration should always be given to alternative ways of achieving a desirable distribution of income.

Compensation. An alternative method of allowing for some of the distributional effects of a project is to compensate those adversely affected. Indeed the basic cost–benefit criterion is that of 'potential Pareto improvement', i.e. if appropriate (lump-sum) redistributions were made, everyone would gain from the project (an actual Pareto improvement). If such redistributions actually are made, then most economists would accept that there has been an unambiguous gain.[1] The payment of such compensation would remove much of the need for distributional weights. In 1972 the British government enacted legislation to compensate the sufferers from major investment projects [81]. This legislation, besides benefiting those involved, gives more weight to environmental effects by converting hypothetical costs into hard financial costs. Nevertheless, from the point of view of the above theory, the legislation is (inevitably) deficient in a number of important respects.

[1] Notwithstanding, the *distribution* of income could have become more unequal if the rich received a disproportionate share of the gains. If welfare depends in part on relative income, overall welfare may actually drop even when there is a Pareto improvement according to the standard criterion.

(i) In practice, not all losses will be compensated in full (eligibility is restricted to certain sorts of development and certain types of effect). Unscrupulous local authorities have a reputation for attempting to impose unfavourable terms and, where the issue is taken to a court, inevitably 'objective' criteria will be employed, which frequently understate the damage; for example houses will be valued at market prices which often understate their value to the occupant by a substantial margin [108].

(ii) Compensation is paid not by the beneficiaries but out of general revenue. Thus there are still losers from the project – namely the tax-payers. The Pareto improvement remains 'potential' and a significant distributional effect remains. If the beneficiaries are relatively affluent, as with road and airport projects, this distributional effect will be adverse.

Finally it should be emphasised that this kind of compensation scheme at best ensures that the project will not *adversely* affect income distribution. By contrast, the use of distributional weights tends to favour schemes which *improve* the distribution of income.

Separate facilities. This provides a means of allowing for variations in environmental tastes. A familiar example is the provision of smoking and non-smoking compartments in trains. It has been proposed that transistors be banned from some beaches and motor transport from large tracts of country [28]. While in essence the case for separate facilities is strong and can lead to an increase in everyone's welfare, there are some important distributional implications.

First, how large should the area of motor-free land be? Clearly this choice crucially affects the distribution between (say) nature lovers and motorists. This issue does not seem to have been considered by environmentalists. *If* nature lovers tend to be more affluent than motorists, then a more general distributional issue arises. In fact, there seems to be an extraordinary view abroad among growth-men [16, 18, 82] that motorists are an impoverished group.

Further problems are raised by residential immobility. For example, while conventional theory tends to suggest that similar rivers should attain a similar level of murkiness (where the

74

marginal cost of extra pollution equals the marginal benefit) the separate facilities argument indicates that the quality of rivers should be deliberately varied; there would then be clean rivers for bathing, fishing and general amenity and dirty rivers for factories and sewage works. Were the same total level of effluents equally distributed among the rivers, fishing and bathing might be possible in none. The principle has been adopted in the Ruhr area of Germany. The quality of the Ruhr is maintained while the Emscher only just satisfies minimum hygiene standards [73]. Zoning regulations in the United Kingdom follow similar principles.

Apart from the obvious advantages of such schemes there are some very unfortunate distributional consequences. One important class of losers from the Ruhr scheme are residents of the Emscher locality. Were income equally distributed and households perfectly mobile this would not matter. People who place a relatively low value on fishing and stream quality will tend to locate near the Emscher. If there is a general preference for high stream quality, then house prices there will be reduced. Since income is most unequally distributed, the residents of the Emscher districts will not be so much 'those who place a relatively low value on stream quality' as 'the poor'. Once again preferences and incomes become entangled in the 'willingness-to-pay' criterion. In such circumstances separate facilities, while catering for variations in preference maps, also frequently involve an unequal distribution of environmental services.

Summary. Environmentalists often claim that arguments for protecting the environment are distribution-free, anti-environmentalists that environmental policies favour the rich. The first claim is misleading, the second wrong.

The range of environmental problems and policies is immense. All groups, rich and poor, are affected. Since the poor generally live and work in the worst environments, there is great scope for projects for environmental improvement with an altogether favourable impact.

The impact of other policies is less favourable. Policies which extend the willingness-to-pay criterion have in particular been condemned as benefiting the rich, although we have found this

75

condemnation to be altogether too sweeping. In any case, environmental policies with adverse distributional effects should not simply be abandoned; we gave several examples of how instead they may be modified to eliminate or at least lessen the adverse impact on distribution.

ENVIRONMENTAL STANDARDS AND THE THIRD WORLD

In this section, we consider the accusation that rich countries are, through international controls or through aid and tariff policies, attempting to impose their own environmental standards on the Third World. Three possible motives for such attempts may be distinguished: protectionism, paternalism, and concern for their own (i.e. the rich countries') environments. These motives are not always easy to disentangle in practice.

Protectionism is pretty universally condemned as a disreputable motive. But there is a genuine fear that environmental arguments may be used as pretexts for a new wave of protectionism. Each case must be judged on its merits. No more can usefully be said here.

Environmental standards may alternatively be imposed in the supposed interests of the Third World itself. This raises two questions. Are rich countries justified in attempting to impose standards? And, if so, what standards are appropriate? The first of these questions has a long history, especially in the controversies over aid. Is paternalism ever justified? Does he who pays the piper have a special right to call the tune? In other words, do donor countries have a moral right to impose conditions to ensure that such aid is used 'wisely' – or, more generally, that 'wise' development policies are pursued? Are they better able than the recipients to judge what constitutes wise policies? And are such conditions efficacious in practice? Since these questions are not especially concerned with the environment, we shall not pursue them here. On the second question (what standards are appropriate?) the view is sometimes expressed that, in poor countries, economic growth is crucial and environmental issues unimportant. The macro-analyses of Chapters 2 and 3 lent only moderate support to these propositions. What

76

these analyses obscure, however, is the enormous variety of environmental problems. It may legitimately be argued that, in conditions of extreme poverty, not too much attention should be lavished on, say, the visual quality of the landscape, but such arguments scarcely apply to soil erosion and the grosser forms of pollution. Many of these constitute threats to health and life at least as serious (and because of extreme poverty, more intractable) as any that exist in the industrialised nations [91, 93]. Environmental problems are in some respects different; their context is different, and different approaches may be required, but they are certainly not unimportant.

Finally, there is an important class of environmental effects which transcends national boundaries [87]. This includes global pollution (e.g. pesticides, some forms of air pollution), indirect pollution through imported goods (e.g. poisoning from lead-painted toys or contaminated goods) and a wide range of phenomena affecting nearby countries (e.g. downstream river pollution). Action in respect of such externalities is in general justified on allocational grounds, although certainly there may be distributional arguments to be considered.

Some of these effects arise from trade in contaminated goods. These may be dealt with quite simply by the importing country by taxing such goods or prohibiting them altogether. Such controls should naturally apply equally to home produced goods; if not 'protectionism' may be suspected. It should not be supposed that such controls are *necessarily* injurious to poor countries; for example, encouragement of natural fibres because of the greater disposal problems of synthetics would benefit primary producers, many of them poor. But in other cases (e.g. contaminated food, unsafe toys), controls may impinge with especial severity on the Third World countries, who may find the new standards especially difficult to meet. Clearly it is generally better in such cases for the rich country concerned to tackle the adverse effect on the Third World country by increasing its aid contribution or reducing protectionist tariffs than by abandoning its environmental control.[1]

[1] The case is complicated by adjustment problems in the poor country. As ever, this constitutes an argument for gradualism (cf. p. 71).

Where the externalities are associated with the production process, it is more difficult to find the appropriate disincentive. Indeed the need for an international body to control international externalities closely parallels the need for governments to control domestic externalities. Again, such controls (e.g. banning D.D.T.) may have an uneven impact. There may sometimes be a case, especially in the short run, for exempting poor countries, but in general it would seem preferable to counter distributional side-effects via multinational distributional policies.[1]

INTERGENERATIONAL EQUITY

The theory of intertemporal choice has always been concerned with intergenerational equity. A major argument for raising the growth rate was that individual decision-makers give insufficient weight to the interests of descendants. This may be attributable quite simply to the selfishness of the current generation. If so, a difficult question arises as to how far even 'immoral' preferences of the 'body politic' should, or in a democracy can, be overridden [31].

However, inadequate provision for descendants has also been attributed to a particular form of market failure known as the Isolation Paradox [109]: it is argued that individuals would perhaps be prepared to bequeath more to future generations if other individuals would agree to do the same; the market provides no mechanism for striking such a contract which must therefore be accomplished through the political process. Furthermore it is established that (on plausible assumptions about an individual's relative valuation of consumption by himself, his contemporaries, his own descendants and their contemporaries) he will save *less than* the socially optimal amount; this conclus-

[1] The case of D.D.T. provides an instructive example. It could be argued that a heavy tax rather than a ban is the allocationally optimal policy. Suppose a heavy tax were combined with transfers to restore the *ex-ante* distribution. Under such a regime it might be that poor countries, given their desperate food shortage, would continue to use D.D.T. despite the tax. If so, the case for employing any ban *selectively* is strong even on allocative grounds.

ion is moreover entirely independent of the relative income of different generations.

This result is indeed paradoxical. It is surprising enough that each generation wishes to bequeath as much as it does to successors who (at least in terms of M-goods) will be so much more affluent (p. 150). It is difficult to see why a considered social judgement should produce a yet larger bequest.[1]

However, the significance of this line of argument is transformed by the environmental considerations discussed in this book. It is possible that, taking E-goods into account, welfare is not growing. Even if it is, it may soon cease to do so in the face of increasing population density and the depletion of productive and environmental resources. This affects the argument in two ways. On the one hand it should greatly heighten our concern for future generations; on the other, raising the growth rate ceases to be an efficacious way of assisting them and may indeed add to their plight.[2]

However the discount rate remains a valid index of our concern for the future. The pro-growth optimists have always considered this excessive. On a pessimistic view of the future, it is surely indefensible.

[1] Individual bequests may be inflated by the following 'socially irrelevant' factors: (a) they may be accidental by-products of saving for one's own purposes (e.g. a house bought primarily for oneself, which, incidentally, one's descendants inherit); (b) they may be a defence against expanding wants and relative income effects; thus one may attempt to bequeath sufficient to maintain one's descendants at least at the same relative position to which their upbringing has accustomed them; if so, the more others save, the more one needs to save oneself. Thus the overall *direction* of bias seems uncertain. But certainly the argument that markets provide an inadequate vehicle for these decisions is well founded.

[2] Note the important possibility that growth increases welfare in the medium term (within the life time of the current generation) but at the cost of a reduction in welfare (or even Doom) in the more distant future.

Appendix
Alternatives to G.N.P.

AN IMPROVED MEASURE OF WELFARE

Environmentalists and others have suggested that G.N.P. and similar national income aggregates are inadequate as welfare measures and hence inappropriate as policy targets. One reaction to this attack is to abandon G.N.P. altogether, except for short-term stabilisation and similar exercises. This however leaves a void in economic targetry which is not easily filled, and an alternative approach is to improve the existing measures.

The principles according to which G.N.P. is constructed are reasonably clear and may be extended, for example, to cover non-marketed activities. The practical difficulties of such an exercise have however always daunted national income accountants, the more especially as a number of more or less arbitrary procedures must be employed. Recently, Nordhaus and Tobin [30] have pioneered an extended measure of American G.N.P. for various years from 1929 to 1965. Their ostensible purpose is to discover whether welfare has in fact risen in recent decades, or whether, as suggested by certain social critics [28], it has moved in the opposite direction to that indicated by G.N.P. However, in so far as their improved measure reflects welfare accurately (and, even more important, without bias), the exercise is of much more than historical significance. For, such a measure, truly representing welfare, could (unlike G.N.P.) appropriately be used as a target of policy.

We will begin by looking at Nordhaus and Tobin's results for the period 1947 to 1965 summarised in Table 2 and then pass to a critical assessment of their derivation and significance.

G.N.P. almost doubled over the period. The more refined measure of output (line 10) and the 'sustainable measure of economic welfare' (line 12) show a growth rate which though much reduced is still substantial. The authors conclude: 'Although G.N.P. and other national income aggregates are imperfect measures of welfare, the broad picture which they convey remains.'

TABLE 2

	1947	1965	1947–65
	\$ billion constant prices		% change
1 G.N.P.	310	618	99
2 Less capital consumption	–18	–55	206
3 N.N.P.	292	563	97
4 Non-market activities	160	295	84
5 Leisure	467	627	34
6 Services of capital	37	79	114
7 *Less* additional capital consumption	–51	–93	82
8 Disamenities	–19	–35	84
9 Instrumental expenditures	–32	–94	194
10 Adjusted output	854	1343	58
11 Less growth requirement	5	–102	..
12 Sustainable 'Measure of Economic Welfare'	859	1241	44

In fact, by far the most significant correction, quantitatively, is for leisure. It will be seen that in 1947, this was the biggest component of Nordhaus and Tobin's final welfare measure, half as big again as G.N.P. While leisure increased over the period, its growth was much less than that of G.N.P. Thus its inclusion brings the overall rate of growth down substantially.[1] In our critique, we shall concentrate exclusively on the envir-

[1] Since 'zero' economic welfare (unlike 'zero' output) is a more or less arbitrary point, *rates* of growth are of little significance.

onmental items (lines 8 and 9) and on certain items which do not appear in the table at all.[1]

Item 8 is a measure of environmental disamenity, and though very difficult to measure, is conceptually straightforward.

Item 9 is described by the authors as 'activities which are not directly sources of utility themselves' but are 'regrettably necessary'; commuting, law and order and defence are cited as examples. Two separate though overlapping issues appear to be involved. First, some expenditures usually regarded as final output may more appropriately be regarded as inputs to the production process. Travelling to work and any government expenditure that benefits industry rather than individuals provide examples.[2] The authors' terminology, and to some extent the items actually included, suggest that they have this primarily in mind.

A rather different point is that expenditures may be under-

---

[1] For completeness, however, the reader may perhaps appreciate the following brief notes on the rest of the table: *Non-market activities* – largely housework and do-it-yourself. There is an interesting discussion on the valuation of both this and *leisure*, and the authors present alternative estimates. *Additional capital* – certain durable items (e.g. private cars) are inappropriately treated as current expenditures in conventional national accounts. The authors reclassify these as investment items, yielding services (item 6) and subject to depreciation (item 7), in line with the present treatment of owner-occupied dwellings. No allowance is made for the consumption of natural resources (see text). The *growth requirement* represents the investment required (i) for additions to the population (this item would be very important in most developing countries) and (ii) to permit future living standards to rise *pro rata* with technical progress. The second adjustment is challenged by Matthews in the discussion which follows the main paper.

[2] There are clearly a host of difficulties. For example, while travel to work is in a sense an input, individuals are the main beneficiaries of any reduction in commuting times. Indeed other expenditures, undertaken by firms, e.g. provision of sports grounds, though conventionally treated as intermediate, are more appropriately regarded as final expenditures. Many government expenditures (e.g. roads) benefit both industry and final consumers and the constituent benefits are extremely difficult to separate.

taken to offset or eliminate a reduction in environmental quality, quite possibly stemming from M-goods production. Clearly it would be wrong to include such expenditures in a welfare measure unless at the same time a deduction is made for the reduction in environmental quality that would otherwise have occurred. Since item 8 relates only to *actual* deteriorations in environmental quality, a further deduction for these expenditures is clearly required.[1]

Perhaps the most striking thing about these items is their small size and rate of growth. Taken together, they grow faster than G.N.P. (153 per cent) but not dramatically so, and at the end of the period constitute a mere 10 per cent of the overall welfare measure.

Let us examine their coverage and derivation. Instrumental expenditures comprise nearly all government current expenditure, together with personal business expenses and one-fifth of personal transport expenditure to cover commuting. Other candidates for consideration include advertising expenditure, private medical bills, garden pesticides and heating bills. The last three items have perhaps led to some improvement in health, gardening and domestic comfort, but are partly a response to increased stress, reduced resistence of bacteria and garden pests and acclimatisation to higher temperatures (too high for health). All these phenomena are the direct result of economic growth. These examples have been cited as relatively objective examples of the Galbraithian phenomenon of want creation. General acceptance of Galbraith's position or of Duesenberry's Relative Income Hypothesis of course makes nonsense of any attempt to measure economic welfare along these lines. Nordhaus and Tobin consider 'the philosophical problems raised by the malleability of consumer wants too deep to be resolved' in their measures. The deficiency is no less fatal for being inevitable.

[1] Abramovitz suggests in discussion that a distinction must be made between expenditures which increase welfare and expenditures which merely offset a deterioration. This criticism seems to be misplaced as far as environmental quality is concerned in that, in principle, actual improvements in environmental quality will be picked up under item 9.

Estimation of the enormous variety of disamenities is obviously a task of gargantuan proportions, in the face of which one can hardly fail to admire Nordhaus and Tobin's desperate expedient of estimating the full sweep of disamenities in one blow in terms of the wage differential between urban and rural areas![1] This approach is justified in the following manner. In a perfect labour market, the *marginal* worker is indifferent between work in the city and in the country: to him the wage difference must exactly equal the various disadvantages of working in the city. Hence, assuming all non-monetary differences between country and city to be environmental, the wage differential provides a measure of the relative disamenity of city working (as perceived by the marginal worker).

At the risk of labouring the obvious, it may be just worth listing a few of the objections to this approach.

(1) Labour markets are peculiarly subject to institutional influences and are never even approximately in equilibrium. Most people are attached to their own localities and have little knowledge of other areas. Not only do they lack the perfect knowledge required of the theory, but are highly immobile. Many workers will be influenced more by job availability and prospects than by wage differentials.[2]

(2) The objection to marginal valuation in this case is particularly strong. The price of a loaf of bread is a measure of (almost) everyone's marginal valuation for (almost) everyone buys bread. But the wage differential in question reflects (at best) the marginal valuation of the most mobile which are

[1] Nordhaus and Tobin note that 'many of the negative "externalities" of economic growth are connected with urbanisation and congestion'. But elsewhere these externalities are accorded the general description 'disamenities' and there is virtually no admission that there might be important additional disamenities not reflected in this measure. The authors distinguish degrees of urbanisation using multiple regression techniques. For expositional purposes the analysis is here spelt out in terms of a simple urban/rural dichotomy.

[2] Nordhaus and Tobin attempt to meet the market disequilibrium difficulty by the inclusion of an additional variable in their regression analyses. This hardly meets the evaluation issues discussed in this paragraph.

scarcely typical of the population at large. Might there perhaps be a correlation between mobility and restlessness and a low valuation of E-goods?

(3) There are many other factors influencing choices between working in the city and the country, such as house prices (and availability). There will also be the largely irrelevant attraction of the social centre of the country or district; even if the town grows in size and squalor, it will still exert this pull.[1]

(4) Disamenity does not relate wholly or even mainly to working conditions. The home environment is probably more important, and environmental conditions associated with travel and recreation are also relevant. This would not matter if those (and their families) who worked in the city (country) also lived and recreated there. As it is, commuting and, to a lesser extent out-of-town trips and holidays allow people to work in the town while avoiding many of the environmental ills. This reduces the wage differential required. It might be argued that the environmental ills of the city are less serious if they can be avoided in these ways. But this brings us back to point (2), that disamenity is being judged by the (affluent) minority who commute.

Nordhaus and Tobin make no deduction for the consumption of natural resources. They justify this omission on the controversial view that 'natural resources [will not] become an increasingly severe drag on economic growth'.[2] The shaky basis for this conclusion was discussed in Chapter 4.

Even on the most optimistic assumptions, however, some deduction should be made for resource consumption. Exhaustion of particular mines, for example, means that resources must be expended finding new mines and possibly transporting the ores over greater distances or in the development of substitute material or resource-augment processes. Dereliction, unemployment and other adaptation problems also frequently

[1] Compare Mishan's [28] discussion of the fashion industry. Being 'in the fashion' is from the individual viewpoint rational enough. But the virtues of any particular fashion can hardly be gauged by adding up the utilities to particular individuals of following it.

[2] They recognise that certain resources in common ownership pose serious problems, especially where their regulation requires international co-operation, but make no adjustment even for these.

follow from the abandonment of one mine in favour of an alternative source. Of course, on a pessimistic view of the future, this form of disinvestment assumes overriding importance.

Perhaps the main value of the Nordhaus–Tobin exercise is to underline the utter hopelessness of extending the national accounts to obtain a statistical measure of welfare.

AN ALTERNATIVE MEASURE OF SOCIO-ECONOMIC DEVELOPMENT

An altogether different reaction to the inadequacies of G.N.P. as a welfare measure is represented by the 'social indicators' movement. This movement rejects the whole idea of measuring welfare in monetary terms as both artificial and distributionally biased.

Of course social indicators have long been used in particular contexts. The interesting question is whether a suitable selection of indicators, either separately or somehow combined, can be used to provide a general picture of a country's socio-economic well-being.

We here give a very summary description of a recent attempt by the United Nations Research Institute for Social Development to construct a single measure of socio-economic development (M.S.E.D.) from eighteen selected indicators [100]. These eighteen indicators were selected from among the much larger number available on the following principles.

(1) *Representativeness* comprising wide coverage of and balance between various aspects of economic and social life. Data availability however imposes severe limits on what can be covered.

(2) *Correlation*. Indicators were chosen which are highly correlated with one another and with an intuitive scale of the development. 'If an indicator does not have a good correlation with other indicators of development, then it must be rejected as a development indicator.'

(3) *Desirability*. Indicators of unambiguously undesirable by-products of development (e.g. industrial pollution), however typical of the development process, were excluded.

Each indicator was converted to an index on a scale 0–100 using statistically derived 'correspondence points' defining a typical pattern of development. Thus, typically, mean life expectancy of x might be found to coexist with protein consumption y and electricity consumption z. These three values are accorded a common number on their respective index scales. The resulting indicators were finally combined using weights reflecting the strength of the correlation between individual indicators and the remaining seventeen.

Some of the indicators used, such as life expectancy (reflecting health) and protein consumption (representing nutrition), reflect basic needs or generally accepted goals. Others, such as electricity and steel consumption, are more closely connected with industrialisation and the manufacture of material goods. Some indicators (such as the percentage urbanised) are described as structural and admitted not to be values in themselves but 'important structural aspects of growth'.

In fact, apart from the rejection of certain indicators under criterion (3), the authors' aim is to construct a scale which reflects not values[1] but a typical pattern of development. In this they are highly successful. All the indicators, though relating to very diverse features of the socio-economic system, are highly intercorrelated and all but one are more closely correlated with the overall index than with G.N.P. A typical pattern of development is very clearly discernible.

An interesting feature of the M.S.E.D. is that countries with an equal income distribution rank more highly than they do using a conventional G.N.P. measure. This is because so many of the indicators reflect basic needs, which do not figure so prominently if a willingness-to-pay criterion (inherent in G.N.P.) is used.

The authors make no claim that the typical pattern of development of even that development itself is desirable – except perhaps in as far as a country's pattern of development reflects the values or at least the (partly politically) revealed preferences of the population. In the main, indeed, the undesirable by-products of development, which have been the concern of this book, have been excluded under criterion (3). Certain environ-

[1] A purely normative approach is explicitly rejected as 'arbitrary', 'capricious' and perhaps even 'contradictory'.

mental effects do creep in: electricity consumption and steel consumption, though inserted to represent industrial development, are also direct measures of resource depletion, while urbanisation is the disamenity effect to which Nordhaus and Tobin give most emphasis. However no attempt is made to distinguish the adverse aspect of these indicators from the favourable.

In one respect only does the M.S.E.D. incorporate environmental effects in a way that G.N.P. does not. The health indicator (alone of the eighteen) is a more basic welfare indicator than any appearing in G.N.P. The latter statistic incorporates expenditures (private or public) to promote health, but no indicator of the state of health itself. If a degraded environment leads to ill-health, this is reflected in the M.S.E.D. but not in G.N.P.[1]

The M.S.E.D., despite its wide coverage and useful features, fails to meet the environmentalists' criticisms of traditional measures. It is not acceptable as a goal of policy – for the same reasons that G.N.P. is not. An M.S.E.D.-maximising government, like a G.N.P.-maximising one, will ignore important aspects of life not adequately reflected in the index. This study can only confirm the feeling that a comprehensive welfare measure is a chimera.[2]

[1] However notice that for this pollution effect to be picked up it is necessary that it be outweighed by some *favourable* feature of development. Were the pollution effect on life expectancy to dominate so that development leads to a reduction in life expectancy, then this indicator is automatically dropped (criterion (3)) and the pollution effect is lost. Notice also that a basic welfare indicator also picks up exogenous influences such as climate.

[2] The M.S.E.D. could be improved by incorporating more basic welfare indicators in place of the intermediate indicators of doubtful welfare significance which at present figure so prominently. Data limitations may however frequently pose insuperable problems. Also the authors' objections to indicators of the adverse by-products of development would appear to be relevant not to the compilation and presentation of such indicators but simply to their incorporation in an *overall* M.S.E.D. The presentation of such indicators would do much to correct an otherwise distorted picture of development. Nevertheless despite these possibilities, the textual comment stands.

Bibliography

GENERAL

[1] J. S. Bain, *Environmental Decay: Economic Causes and Remedies* (Little, Brown, Boston, 1973).

[2] P. Bohm and A. V. Kneese (eds), *The Economics of Environment* (Macmillan, London, 1971) (reprinted from *Swedish Journal of Economics*, 1971).

[3] École Pratique des Hautes Études, *Political Economy of Environment, Problems of Method* (Mouton, Paris, 1972).

[4] M. Edel, *Economies and the Environment* (Prentice-Hall, Englewood Cliffs, 1973).

[5] A. C. Enthoven and A. M. Freeman (eds) *Pollution, Resources, and the Environment* (Norton, New York, 1973).

[6] A. M. Freeman III *et al.*, *The Economics of Environmental Policy* (Wiley, New York, 1973).

[7] Institute of Fiscal Studies, *Proceedings of a Conference on Fiscal Policy and the Environment* (London, 1974).

[8] H. Jarrett (ed.), *Environmental Quality in a Growing Economy*, Resources for the Future (Johns Hopkins, Baltimore, 1966).

[9] W. A. Johnson and J. Hardesty (eds), *Economic Growth vs. the Environment* (Wadsworth, Belmont, 1971).

[10] A. V. Kneese *et al.* (eds), *Managing the Environment: International Economic Cooperation for Pollution Control* (Praeger, New York, 1971).

[11] A. V. Kneese and B. T. Bower (eds), *Environmental Quality Analysis*, Resources for the Future (Johns Hopkins, Baltimore, 1972).

[12] O.E.C.D., *Problems of Environmental Economics* (Paris, 1972).

[13] N. Pole (ed.), *Environmental Solutions* (Cambridge University Conservation Society, Eco-publications, 1972).

[14] S. H. Schurr (ed.), *Energy, Economic Growth and the Environment*, Resources for the Future (Johns Hopkins, Baltimore, 1972).

89

[15] W. Beckerman, 'The Desirability of Economic Growth' in *Conflicts Among Policy Objectives*, ed. N. Kaldor (Blackwell, Oxford, 1971).

[16] W. Beckerman, 'Why We Need Economic Growth', *Lloyds Bank Review* (Nov 1971).

[17] K. E. Boulding, 'Fun and Games with the G.N.P. – the Role of Misleading Calculations in Social Policy' in *The Environmental Crisis*, ed. H. W. Helfrich (Yale University Press, 1970).

[18] A. Crosland, *A Social Democratic Britain*, Fabian Tract 404 (London, 1971).

[19] D. Donaldson and P. Victor, 'On the Dynamics of Air Pollution Control', *Canadian Journal of Economics* (1970).

[20] R. Easterlin, 'Does Economic Growth Improve the Human Lot? Some Empirical Evidence', in *Nations and Households in Economic Growth*, ed. P. A. David and M. W. Reder (Stanford University Press, California, forthcoming).

[21] W. Heller, 'Coming to Terms with Growth and the Environment' in [14] (reprinted in [5]).

[22] N. H. Jacoby and F. G. Pennance, *The Polluters: Industry or Government?*, Institute of Economic Affairs Occasional Paper 36 (London, 1972).

[23] A. V. Kneese, 'The Economics of Environmental Management in the United States', in [10].

[24] J. R. C. Lecomber, *The Growth Objective* (International Institute of Social Economics, Patrington, Emmasglen, 1975).

[25] J. R. C. Lecomber, 'Growth, Externalities and Satisfactions: a Reply to Beckerman', *International Journal of Social Economics* (1974).

[26] M. Lipton, *Assessing Economic Performance* (Staples, London, 1968).

[27] R. N. McKean, 'Growth vs. no Growth', *Daedalus* (1973).

[28] E. J. Mishan, *The Costs of Economic Growth* (Staples, London, 1967).

[29] E. J. Mishan, 'Economic Growth: the Need for Scepticism', *Lloyds Bank Review* (October 1972).

[30] National Bureau of Economic Research, *Economic Growth* (Columbia University Press, 1972).

[31] E. S. Phelps, *Fiscal Neutrality toward Economic Growth* (McGraw-Hill, New York, 1965).

[32] M. J. Roberts, 'On Reforming Economic Growth', *Daedalus* (1973).

[33] M. Stewart, *Labour and the Economy: a Socialist Strategy*, Fabian Tract 413 (London, 1972).

[34] J. Tobin, 'Economic Growth as an Objective of Policy', *American Economic Review, Papers and Proceedings* (1964).

MODELS OF PRODUCTION AND ENVIRONMENT

[35] R. C. d'Arge, 'Economic Growth and the Natural Environment', in [11].

[36] R. C. d'Arge, 'Essay on Economic Growth and Environmental Quality', in [2].

[37] R. C. d'Arge and K. C. Kogiku, 'Economic Growth and the Environment', *Review of Economic Studies* (1973).

[38] P. Nijkamp and J. Paelinck, 'Some Models for the Economic Evaluation of the Environment', *Regional and Urban Studies* (1973).
See also [19] [30] [67].

ON GLOBAL CATASTROPHE

[39] Sir E. Ashby, *et al.*, *Nuisance or Nemesis: a Report on the Control of Pollution* (H.M.S.O., London, 1972).

[40] K. E. Boulding, 'The Economics of the Coming Spaceship Earth' in [8] (reprinted in [5] and [9]).

[41] S. Brubaker, *To Live on Earth*, Resources for the Future, (Johns Hopkins, Baltimore, 1972).

[42] B. Commoner, *The Closing Circle* (Jonathan Cape, London, 1971).

[43] H. E. Daly (ed.), *Toward a Steady-State Economy* (W. H. Freeman, San Francisco, 1973).

[44] P. R. Ehrlich and A. H. Ehrlich, *Population, Resources, Environment* (W. H. Freeman, San Francisco, 1970).

[45] M. T. Farvar and J. P. Milton (eds), *The Careless Technology: Ecology and International Development* (Doubleday, New York, 1973).

[46] E. Goldsmith (ed.), *Blueprint for Survival* (Penguin, Harmondsworth, 1973) (reprinted from *Ecologist* 1972).

[47] J. Maddox, *The Doomsday Syndrome* (Macmillan, London, 1972).

[48] Massachusetts Institute of Technology, *Man's Impact on the Global Environment: Assessment and Recommendations for Action* (M.I.T. Press, 1970).
See also [49–55].

THE MEADOWS MODEL AND CRITICISMS

[49] D. H. Meadows *et al.*, *The Limits to Growth* ([Earth Island], London, 1972).

[50] W. Beckerman, 'Economists, Scientists and Environmental Catastrophe', *Oxford Economic Papers* (1972).

[51] J. Bray, *The Politics of Environment*, Fabian Tract 412 (London, 1972).

[52] H. S. D. Cole *et al.*, *Thinking About the Future: A Critique of The Limits to Growth* (Chatto & Windus, London, 1973) (reprinted from *Futures* 1973).

[53] J. E. Meade, 'Economic Policy and the Threat of Doom' in B. Benjamin, *et al.* (eds), *Resources and Population* (Academic Press, London, 1973).

[54] D. L. Meadows *et al.*, 'The Limits to Growth Controversy: a Response to Sussex', *Futures* (1973).

[55] W. D. Nordhaus, 'World Dynamics: Measurement without Data', *Economic Journal* (1973).
See also [62] [63].

PRODUCTIVE RESOURCES

[56] H. J. Barnett and C. Morse, *Scarcity and Growth* (Johns Hopkins, Baltimore, 1963).

[57] F. Christy Jr and A. D. Scott, *The Common Wealth in Ocean*

Fisheries, Resources for the Future (Johns Hopkins, Baltimore, 1965).

[58] M. S. Common and D. W. Pearce, 'Adaptive Mechanisms, Growth, and the Environment; the Case of Natural Resources', *Canadian Journal of Economics* (1973).

[59] P. Dasgupta and G. Heal, 'The Optimal Depletion of Exhaustible Resources', *Review of Economic Studies* (1974).

[60] P. Dasgupta and G. Heal, *The Economics of Exhaustible Resources* (Cambridge University Press, forthcoming).

[61] H. Hotelling, 'The Economics of Exhaustible Resources', *Journal of Political Economy* (1931).

[62] J. A. Kay and J. A. Mirrlees, 'The Desirability of Natural Resource Depletion' in D. W. Pearce (ed.), *The Economics of Natural Resource Depletion* (Macmillan, forthcoming).

[63] J. R. C. Lecomber, 'Growth, Resources and Taxation', in [7].

[64] National Academy of Sciences and Natural Resources Council, *Resources and Man* (W. H. Freeman, San Francisco, 1969).

[65] V. L. Smith, 'Economics of Production from Natural Resources', *American Economic Review* (1968).

[66] R. Solow, 'Intergenerational Equity and Exhaustible Resources', *Review of Economic Studies* (1974).

[67] N. Vousden, 'Basic Theoretical Issues of Resource Depletion', *Journal of Economic Theory* (1973).

POLLUTION AND ITS CONTROL

[68] R. U. Ayres and A. V. Kneese, 'Production, Consumption and Externalities', *American Economic Review* (1969).

[69] W. J. Baumol and W. E. Oates, 'The Uses of Standards and Prices for Protection of the Environment', in [2].

[70] J. Bugler, *Polluting Britain* (Penguin, Harmondsworth, 1972).

[71] M. I. Goldman, *Ecology and Economics: Controlling Pollution in the 70s* (Prentice-Hall, Englewood Cliffs, 1967).

[72] W. F. Kapp, *The Social Costs of Business Enterprise* (Harvard University Press, 1950).

[73] A. V. Kneese, 'Water Quality Management by Regional Authorities in the Ruhr Area', *Papers and Proceedings of the Regional Science Association* (1963) (reprinted in [71]).

[74] A. V. Kneese, 'Background for the Economic Analysis of Environmental Pollution', in [2].

[75] M. R. Langham *et al.*, 'Agricultural Pesticides: Productivity and Externalities', in [11].

[76] D. W. Pearce, 'An Incompatibility in Planning for a Steady State and Planning for Maximum Economic Welfare', *Environment and Planning* (1973).

[77] I. Sachs, 'Approaches to a Political Economy of Environmental Disruption', in [3].

[78] P. A. Victor, *The Economics of Pollution* (Macmillan, London, 1972).
See also [15] [22] [28] [32] [39] [46].

DISTRIBUTIONAL ISSUES

[79] S. Andic and A. T. Peacock, 'The International Distribution of Income, 1949 and 1957', *Journal of the Royal Statistical Society* (Series A, 1961).

[80] W. Beckerman and R. Bacon, 'The International Distribution of Income', in *Unfashionable Economics: Essays in Honour of Lord Balogh*, ed. P. Streeten (Weidenfeld & Nicolson, London, 1970).

[81] Department of the Environment, *Development and Compensation: Putting People First*, Cmnd 5124 (H.M.S.O., London, 1972).

[82] A. Downs, 'The Political Economy of Improving our Environment', in [1].

[83] J. S. Duesenberry, *Income, Saving and the Theory of Consumer Behaviour* (Harvard University Press, 1947).

[84] A. M. Freeman III, 'The Distribution of Environmental Quality', in [11].

[85] W. R. Johnson, 'Should the Poor Buy No Growth?', *Daedalus* (1973).

[86] D. W. Pearce, 'Is Ecology Elitist?', *Ecologist* (1973).
See also [16] [24] [29] [33] [42] [44] [52] [66] [105] [110].

DEVELOPING COUNTRIES

[87] W. J. Baumol, *Environmental Protection, International Spillovers and Trade* (Almquist & Wiksell, Stockholm, 1971).

[88] L. Brown, 'Rich Countries and Poor in a Finite Interdependent World', *Daedalus* (1973).

[89] M. Clawson, 'Economic Development and Environmental Impact: International Aspects', in [3].

[90] R. C. d'Arge, 'Trade, Environmental Controls and the Developing Countries', in [12].

[91] R. F. Dasmann *et al.*, *Ecological Principles for Economic Development* (Wiley, London, 1973).

[92] Institute of Development Studies, *Bulletin* (University of Sussex, 1971).

[93] I. Sachs, 'Environmental Quality Management and Development Planning: Some Suggestions for Action', in [95].

[94] R. G. Wilkinson, *Poverty and Progress* (Methuen, London, 1973).

[95] United Nations, Conference on the Human Environment, *Development and Environment* (Founex Report) (U.N., Geneva, 1972).
See also [42] [45] [52] [79] [80] [100].

MISCELLANEOUS REFERENCES

[96] E. Denison, *Why Growth Rates Differ* (Brookings, Washington D.C., 1968).

[97] R. Dubos, *Man Adapting* (Yale University Press, 1971).

[98] J. K. Galbraith, *The Affluent Society* (Hamilton, London, 1958).

[99] Sir R. Harrod, *Reforming the World's Money* (Macmillan, London, 1965).

[100] D. V. McGranahan *et al.*, *Concepts and Measurement of Socio-economic Development*, U.N. Research Institute of Social Development (Praeger, New York, 1972).

[101] J. E. Meade, *The Growing Economy* (Allen & Unwin, London, 1968).

[102] National Academy of Sciences, *Rapid Population Growth:*

Causes and Policy Implications (Johns Hopkins, Baltimore, 1971).

[103] F. W. Notestein, 'Zero Population Growth: What Is It?', *Family Planning Perspectives* (1970).

[104] E. P. Odum, *Ecology* (Holt, Rinehart & Winston, New York, 1963).

[105] D. W. Pearce, *Cost–Benefit Analysis* (Macmillan, London, 1971).

[106] M. Peston, *Public Goods and the Public Sector* (Macmillan, London, 1972).

[107] A. C. Pigou, *The Economics of Welfare* (Macmillan, London, 1924).

[108] Commission on the Third London Airport, *Report* (Roskill Report) (H.M.S.O., London, 1971).

[109] A. K. Sen, 'On Optimising the Rate of Saving', *Economic Journal* (1961).

[110] C. Sharp, 'Congestion and Welfare: an Examination of the Case for a Congestion Tax', *Economic Journal* (1966).

[111] R. H. Strotz, 'Myopia and Inconsistency in Dynamic Utility Maximisation', *Review of Economic Studies* (1956).

[112] A. Toffler, *Future Shock* (Bodley Head, New York, 1970).

[113] A. A. Walters, 'The Theory and Measurement of the Private and Social Cost of Congestion', *Econometrica* (1961). Reprinted in D. Munby (ed.), *Transport Economics* (Penguin, Harmondsworth, 1968).

2421